Teaching

Also available from Continuum

How to Design a Training Course, Peter Taylor

English Language Teacher's Handbook, Joanna Baker and Heather Westrup

Teaching Teachers

Processes and Practices

Angi Malderez and Martin Wedell

continuum

Continuum International Publishing Group
The Tower Building   80 Maiden Lane, Suite 704
11 York Road   New York, NY
London   10038
SE1 7NX

www.continuumbooks.com

British Library Cataloguing-in-Publication Data
A catalogue record for this book is available from the British Library.

ISBN: 0 8264 8490 5 (hardback)
      0 8264 8491 3 (paperback)

Library of Congress Cataloguing-in-Publication Data
A catalog record for this book is available from the Library of Congress.

Typeset by YIIT Ltd, London
Printed and bound in Great Britain by The Cromwell Press, Trowbridge, Wiltshire

Contents

Acknowledgements

We owe a debt of gratitude to all those teachers becoming teachers of teachers with whom we have worked in the last decade for the opportunities they gave us to develop and articulate the ideas presented here. In particular thanks to ISAs and RESCies in Sri Lanka, PSMAs and TOTSies in Botswana, PETTsters in China and mentors and mentor trainers in Hungary, Romania and Latvia.

We are also very grateful to Professor Peter Tomlinson, friend, colleague and mentor, for his invaluable comments on an early draft.

Thanks, too, to colleagues from Continuum (Anthony Haynes who commissioned the book, and Christina Garbutt who guided it to its conclusion), and from the TESOL group in the School of Education who kept the wheels turning while we were writing this on study leave.

Finally love and thanks for everything to our families, and in particular to Gary Jeff and Jan.

Glossary

Learners: the teacher or teachers being supported by ToTs.

Mentoring: one-to-one ToTing, most often work-place based, as opposed to ToTing a group of teachers away from their workplace.

Mentor: ToT working one-to one with a teacher.

Mentee: teacher participant in one-to-one.

Pupils: schoolchildren or students in schools or colleges (being taught by the learners whom ToTs teach).

TL programme: Teacher Learning programme. These are the types of programmes taught by ToTs and attended by learners.

ToTs: teachers of teachers – those who support one or more teachers in their learning ToTing.

ToTing: teaching teachers.

We the authors (rather than a 'we' intended to include the reader).

General Introduction

Who this book is for

This book is mainly intended for teachers who are about to adopt or have recently adopted a further role: that of supporting the learning of other future or current teachers. We, of course, hope that more experienced teachers of teachers (ToTs) might also find food for thought or practical ideas in these pages. This 'supporting the learning' of other teachers may involve a range of duties such as:

- being responsible for staff development within the context of a school
- being asked to run a one-off workshop or a longer in-service programme
- starting a new job in an initial teacher preparation programme, or
- agreeing to receive a trainee in their class during the classroom-based elements of their initial teacher qualification programme

In addition, there are a range of other education professionals who may be involved with the provision of programmes for teachers who might find parts of this book helpful. For example, those intending to set up support systems for teachers at a local level during the implementation phases of new regional or national educational initiatives might also find it relevant. Furthermore, while primarily intended for practitioners, this book may also be helpful for those needing to ensure effective dissemination of research findings to teachers, and be a useful addition to reading lists on academic programmes relating to teacher education, educational change and general capacity building in educational development settings.

Who we are

Why does it matter that you have some idea who we are? We believe it matters for several reasons.

First of all we see writing and reading as a dialogue at a distance. It is hard to have a decent conversation with somebody you do not know at all, since one of the main social reasons for any dialogue on any topic is to identify similarities and differences between yourself and the person you are talking to.

Secondly, in assessing how far you agree or disagree with what you read here, or in understanding why we say what we say, it is helpful for you to have some understanding of the experiences that have led us to say it. In other words you need to know something about the experiences of teaching teachers and reading about and researching teacher learning on which we base the statements we make, in order to help you decide whether or to what extent what we say is convincing.

We hope that, if you disagree with what we say, or find your experience has been very different from ours, you do not throw the book away, but rather, as in the story of the blind men and the elephant (see Chapter 1), remain open to the potential usefulness of a new perspective. Conversely, if you find that what we say does not correspond to what you think, we hope you won't automatically feel that you are 'wrong'. We can only offer one perspective, and would be very glad if you were able to help us get a clearer picture through having access to yours. We have included our email addresses in the final chapter and would be genuinely interested to hear from you.

So after all that, who are we? Together we have forty-plus years' experience of teaching teachers in various parts of the world, on all continents apart from Australasia and North America. Before that, or simultaneously, during the early years of teaching teachers, we were both teachers of English as a Foreign language, in state and private settings overseas and in the UK and have a combined total of about 30 years in this role. We are as you can see not youngsters, (and) while some of you might feel we are out of touch or 'past it', hopefully other readers might find this, our age, reassuring! However, we will also argue that it is not merely years of experience that makes what somebody says trustworthy, but also what they have learned from that experience.

The job we both do now is an academic one, which involves us in researching (in the fields of teacher education – for one of us – and educational change – for the other), as well as in teaching teachers, both on formal accredited programmes and within the context of educational development initiatives in various parts of the world.

Why we have written the book

We have written this book for three main reasons. The first is because teachers (becoming ToTs) with whom we have worked over the past decade have asked us to. During this work neither we, nor they, have been able to find any single, accessible source of ideas and practices to support the initial stages of their work as ToTs. We think the main reason they wanted such a book had to do with their need to feel confident and supported as they tried to make their early experiences of teaching teachers successful. We hope that any of you who are beginning in this role will find that what follows is indeed accessible and supportive of your early experiences.

Secondly, the start of this millennium has coincided with education systems being increasingly seen as a key means of raising citizens' skills levels in order to meet the economic challenges of globalization. Consequently, educational reforms of various kinds are happening within many national education systems. The effective teaching of teachers is *the* key factor influencing the extent to which the effective implementation of new education policies and curriculum reforms takes place as intended. This in turn depends on educational reformers' understanding of what such effective teaching of teachers involves. We hope that this book will also provide a resource for such readers.

Finally, we believe that the effective teaching of teachers is the most efficient form of dissemination for many educational research findings. For reasons which we hope will become clearer in Part 1, simply telling teachers about relevant research findings, whether through writing or lectures/presentations, is unlikely to affect what many or even most of the listeners or readers actually do once back in their classrooms. We therefore believe that issues discussed in this book are of relevance to, for example, university lecturers hoping to disseminate their own or others' research findings through their teaching of teachers on accredited (BA, MA) or non-accredited courses, as well as to those working on educational research projects who genuinely want or need to disseminate findings to teachers.

What's in the book

As you will see later, we do not believe that either learning to teach, or learning to teach teachers is as simple a matter as doing as you are told or 'applying theories'. So why are we seeming to start this book with a section that deals with, in effect, 'theories'? There are two answers to this question. The first is that what we present in Part 1 we see as conceptual tools to use in the practices of planning and preparing to teach. By conceptual tools we mean practical ways of thinking about your practices as a ToT. The ones we describe here are the ones we use ourselves. Secondly, in any dialogue it is necessary to have a shared language. Therefore through discussing these theories we are developing a linguistic shorthand for sometimes complex ideas which we will be able to use later in the book when, for example, providing a rationale for a particular practice.

Part 2 discusses the sorts of thinking stages and associated activities we go through when undertaking the 'before teaching' processes of designing, planning and preparing both for programmes with groups of teachers and for one-to-one teaching of teachers (what others call 'mentoring'). The example we use is that of a short in-service programme and we refer back to this to illustrate points elsewhere in the book. We have chosen to use a short in-service programme, first because we feel it is likely to be relevant to more readers and secondly for reasons of space. However, we believe that these ways of thinking about our practices as ToTs are also relevant to longer or initial teacher preparation programmes.

Because we believe that our core practice as ToTs is as much about our own learning as it is about how we behave in our actual teaching, Part 3 is concerned both with ways ToTs can manage their own learning to become more effective managers of others' learning, and with actual teaching behaviour. In this way we see this Part as the next stage in a process, a chronological sequence of practices going from designing, planning and preparing (Part 2) to actual teaching.

Part 4 deals with the final practices in this sequence: assessment and evaluation. Here we consider some of the issues, difficulties and challenges in assessing the learners on programmes, and in evaluating programmes and those who teach on them.

At the end of each Part we make a few suggestions for some additional readings which expand, explain or exemplify ideas discussed in the Part. We explain which sections we feel are relevant and why we have chosen them. Many of these sources inevitably come from our own language education background. However, we hope that you are not put off by the 'language' in the titles, as we have chosen readings that we think are of relevance to teachers of any subject (including 'teaching').

Ways of using the book

If you are a (new) teacher of teachers

We start with a section called Preparing Yourself (Part 1), because preparing your own thinking is crucial to your ultimate effectiveness (for reasons we explain in the section itself), and because in the remainder of the book we draw on ideas introduced here. This, in some ways, is quite a complex section and there are two reasons why you might not want to read through all of it initially.

If you are in a hurry

If you are in a hurry and working at a particular stage of the sequence outlined above, you may want to go straight to the relevant Part/chapter. We do, though, suggest you visit Part 1 as soon as you can and perhaps even revisit it after your early experiences of teaching teachers, when you may find it makes a new and different sense. In other words, although we hope this book is one which can be dipped into as and when needed, there is quite a bit of cross-referencing within it, and so a quick read from beginning to end would help you to understand some of the important connections that we try to make.

If you get stuck

Some readers may 'get stuck' while reading Part 1. In this case we suggest you move on to Part 2 and return to specific sections of Part 1 as they are referred to in later chapters. When you have completed the book, and perhaps had a little experience of ToTing, you may find Part 1 is more accessible.

If you are involved in instigating educational reforms at a national or local level

While Part 2 of the book may seem of most immediate relevance, this is based on ideas introduced in Part 1. It may also seem less urgent to consider assessment and evaluation (Part 4); however, decisions made very early on in the designing/ planning sequence impact on these practices, and choices made about the means of assessment/evaluation in turn influence design decisions. Finally, although you may not be personally involved in the teaching of teachers and Part 3 may appear less relevant, understanding what is involved in becoming, being and growing as an effective ToT may also influence aspects of your designs or plans.

If you are involved in dissemination of educational research findings

One of the principal audiences for the dissemination of educational research findings is teachers. Such dissemination may take place on accredited courses, or through other, frequently one-off, types of events. However, exposure to findings does not in itself guarantee practical impact: the manner in which teachers are exposed to findings matters. This book suggests one perspective on why it matters, as well as an approach to teaching teachers in more transformative ways.

If you are responsible for an academic course on teacher education

This text is not written in a conventionally academic style, since it is aiming at a practitioner (whole-mind, rather than simply d-mode – see Part 1) readership. Nonetheless, we feel it could prove a useful text on courses about teacher education for three reasons: it provides an overview of the stages in the practical provision of teacher education; it provides a source of starter references for a range of fields within the area; and, because it is designed for a practitioner readership, it potentially provides a bridge to more academic study for practitioner students.

If you are in a development group with other ToTs

Part 3 makes explicit suggestions about a range of activities that your group might find useful. Among these is a 'reading group', and this text, or sections of it, might be the focus of one or more of these sessions.

What we mean by 'teachers' (of teachers)

In the Glossary we have listed some of the terms we will frequently use in this book. Part 1 also introduces key language (and the ideas behind that language) that we will use in subsequent Parts. However, before we start that we want to say something about what we mean by one fundamental word that it is very easy for everyone to assume they understand. This is the word *teacher*. When you hear or read this word, what do you think of? What immediately springs to mind? All over the world, this word is understood, at least by people not in the profession, in very similar ways, although details may be different according to context. For most people, a teacher works in a room and talks to a number of (usually younger) people who listen and 'learn'; a teacher is in charge, is more powerful than the listeners; a teacher 'knows more' than the listeners; a teacher, not the listeners, makes decisions about what happens in the room, and about whether the listeners now know what has been 'taught'. And so on. Most of this is *not* what we mean when we use the word 'teacher' (and teach and teaching) throughout this book. Rather, by teacher we mean someone who provides learners with opportunities for learning (and in the process learns themselves), plans with 'learning promotion potential' in mind (Tomlinson 1995*); accepts that the learners already 'know' a lot which will be useful to the learning endeavour; notices the stages learners have reached, and the successes and difficulties the learners are having and uses this to guide decisions about how best to be supportive. What these two descriptions share is a view of the teacher as a person whose job it is to enable others' learning to occur. The two views differ greatly, however, in their descriptions of what teachers do to support learning, which in turn suggests two very different underlying views of learning.

We recognize that the way we have described our meaning of 'teacher' and 'teaching' is frequently found in articles, books and lectures relating to contemporary ideas about education including teacher education (often using terms such as 'facilitator', or 'trainer' for example). In choosing to use the terms 'teacher' and 'teaching' in talking about ToTs and what they do we are reclaiming the central meaning of teacher as a promoter of learning. Although as we have said the literature describes, for example, what teacher educators/facilitators/trainers might be like and what they might do in very general terms, it is rare to find practical detail on what this might mean for the process and practices of teaching teachers (ToTing). We hope that this book will help demonstrate the sorts of activities that a ToT who shares our view of what a teacher is and does, can practically engage in (when thinking, designing, planning, preparing and then actually teaching, assessing and evaluating) to make the rhetoric reality.

In discussing what we mean by the word 'teacher' we have already begun one of the main preparatory tasks that a ToT needs to undertake – that is, working out what they think and why. Part 1, therefore, which introduces various ideas about, for example, the possible goals of teacher learning and processes which might lead to their achievement, will also we hope serve as a tool to help you explore your own thinking.

*See References, p. 40.

Part 1

Preparing Yourself

Introduction
Preparing your own thinking: why it matters

In trying to answer the question implied above about why it matters how you think, we'd like to start with a couple of stories about our early experiences which you may find more or less similar to your own.

Story 1

In the summer of 1969, when I was nineteen years old, I got a job teaching English on a summer school for young adults. I soon discovered that just being a native speaker of the language was not enough. First of all, there were ways in which I didn't know the language at all: I had to work hard to find ways of describing to myself how it worked and how it was made up, as well as on deciding what parts of that description I would use with my students. To start with, not very consciously I used, or tried to use, ways of working I remembered my language teachers using with me. I eventually discovered that these were not meeting the hopes and expectations of my paying and very vocal learners, and I was very bored. I searched in the growing mass of textbooks and supplementary materials for new ideas. This, however, caused me new problems. I realized I didn't really know why I was selecting what I was to use apart from a belief that the activities might keep my learners temporarily happy and engaged. I needed to be able to convince them, and myself, that what I chose for them to do would actually help them learn and, to do this, I needed to understand much, much more about strategies, processes and conditions which support language learning. In order to do this I went off and got myself a string of TESOL qualifications, each of which made me realize that there was yet more to know!

Story 2

Some years and lots of learning later (with and for my students as well as on courses), my students were generally happy and their results were good. I was asked to work on a 'refresher course' for teachers. I was flattered! And very soon perplexed as well as rather depressed. My teaching of teachers was not as successful as my teaching of language learners had become. With hindsight I can see that as a novice I had again modelled my work on how I had been taught (on the various teacher qualification-getting programmes I had followed), and found it didn't 'work' in ways I or my learners wanted or needed. Once again there was more to learn, and I realized I was back at the start of a new learning journey. I had a different 'subject' to learn about. Instead of the English language my subject was now 'teaching'. Instead of needing to understand and be able to use the strategies and processes, or establish conditions that would support language learning I now needed to understand and be able to use the strategies, processes and conditions that would support teacher learning. Instead of understanding the various different characteristics of the learners I had taught (age, nationalities, first languages, motivations and so on), I needed to understand teachers (their educational and cultural backgrounds, teaching experiences, attitudes, beliefs, motivations and so on).

Many people reading Story 1 may not immediately relate to the situation. They will see differences between their experiences and those of the novice in Story 1. In particular, non-native speaker language teachers will have had to work hard to develop confidence in their own proficiency in the language to be taught. On the other hand, since they will have learnt the second language as a subject, they will probably have had a better explicit understanding of the language structure than the native speaker teacher had.

These days in many parts of the world there is a greater awareness that just because someone is proficient in the skills of the subject to be taught (whether language use, performing mathematical computations, or practising as a scientist) this will not be enough to make them an effective teacher. The novice in Story 1 might therefore not nowadays be hired solely on the basis of subject proficiency.

However, as you are reading this book, we expect that more of you will recognize the scenario in Story 2. This is because, while there is a developing awareness that subject proficiency *is not* sufficient to ensure effective teaching, there remains an assumption that expertise as a subject teacher *is* sufficient to be an effective teacher of teachers.

So why have we started with these (our true, autobiographical) stories? There are many reasons, and these will be discussed in more detail in later chapters. The point here is that Story 2 in particular illustrates a route taken by many ToTs, who, on the basis of their own expertise in teaching, are asked to help others to develop similar expertise.

We will look a little more closely at the parallels between the two stories. As indicated above, in both stories, the teacher is proficient in the skills to be taught (i.e. language use and teaching). In addition, proficiency in these skills was developed over considerable amounts of time. This development occurred as much through experience of 'use of skills in real contexts' as through planned explicit 'learning'.

In both stories, the fact that the teacher was seen to be proficient in the skills to be taught was the basis for appointment. However, the teacher soon, in both cases, realized (even if those who had made the appointment didn't) that although these skills were a necessary starting point, they were not alone going to be sufficient for the teacher to work effectively. In both stories the teacher discovered a need to know more about the subject to be taught and the conditions, processes and strategies which might support others in learning it.

So why did the teacher feel the need to know more? This feeling was born from a lack of confidence, which in turn resulted in part from not being able to justify or explain intuitive decisions made inside and out of the classroom. All teachers need to feel confidence in what they are doing because it has consequences for effectiveness. Feeling knowledgeable can promote that confidence. So the first reason for why what you know and what you do with what you know (how you think) matters is:

> Knowing more about your reasons for doing things in classrooms can make you feel more confident.

Apart from giving you confidence there are also other important practical reasons why knowledge is useful. These relate to the process of making informed (and confident) decisions about what to do when, and how to do it. ToTs may need to make such decisions when, for example:

- designing contextually relevant programmes
- selecting and sequencing and/or designing materials
- effectively supporting teacher learning in a variety of situations
- assessing the outcomes of teacher learning for reasons of accountability or in order to plan the next steps of a course process

These practices differ from those expected of the majority of teachers in schools. While for teachers of school subjects, syllabuses are usually designed and planned by others and materials are frequently pre-prepared or provided in the form of textbooks, there are few pre-designed courses and/or materials for ToTs to use with their learners, particularly for in-service work. This therefore means that many ToTs, in addition to acquiring new knowledge (about the new subject – teaching, and the processes, strategies and conditions which support its learning) also need to develop new skills for new practices (such as designing courses) using new knowledge in what may be new ways for them.

Having relevant information about, for example, teacher knowledge and teacher learning potentially helps ToTs make more appropriate decisions in everything they need to do as a teacher of teachers.

In the next two chapters then we will introduce ideas about what teachers need to know and how they come to know it that we have found of practical use in making our own decisions about how to support the processes of teacher learning.

Chapter 1

What teachers need to learn

Introduction

Arguably what anyone needs to learn depends on three things:

- what the ultimate goal of the learning is
- what they already know, or can do, and
- what the particular aims of a course or programme are

We'll discuss the ways of finding out what teachers already know and can do in Chapter 4, and will consider the importance of knowing this throughout many of the subsequent chapters. The aims of a particular course or programme will be derived from both a view of the ultimate goal in a particular context, and an understanding of teachers' needs. The aims also have to take into account issues to do with resources (time, places, money). These will be discussed further in Part 2. In this chapter we intend to explore possible ways in which the goal of teacher learning can be understood, because this will make a difference to what we think teachers might need to learn, and will affect many other decisions we make.

We'll start by trying to illustrate what we mean by different 'ultimate' aims or goals for learning with another example from our own experience in language education.

One way of thinking about the ultimate goal of language teaching views it as enabling pupils to know about the language (its rules and systems) to almost the same level as the teacher. Another way considers the ultimate goal as enabling them not only to know about language but also to become able to read, write, speak and listen in the foreign language. A further goal is described as communicative competence, where explicit knowledge about the language system and language skills both support the learning of the ability to communicate in the foreign language. Finally there are some teachers who have as their goal to produce competent communicators in the foreign language, a goal that, in addition, takes account of individual learners and the particular meanings they want to express or understand.

We hope any teacher reader will be able to see that the different ways of thinking about the ultimate goal in language teaching will make a considerable difference to the kinds of things that happen in classrooms and the kind of things teachers believe it is important for students to learn. For example, we think there could be considerable amounts of teacher-fronted 'plenary' explanations if a teacher held the first view described above, and a great deal of unpredictable pupil–pupil interaction if a teacher held the last view.

We believe there will similarly be different ways of thinking about ultimate aims for any school subject, which will drive different approaches to teaching and lead to different emphases in the syllabus and so the content of lessons.

A feature of such ultimate goals is that they are often not explicitly stated or written anywhere. For example, language teachers we have seen and talked to haven't actually told us they thought that the ultimate aim of their work was that students should be able to repeat grammar rules and produce sentences including examples of these rules. However, the way that they taught, and what they did in their classes, suggested that this was so (or at least, that the system, as manifest by the design of high-stakes language exams, seemed to hold this view). Similarly many curriculum documents do not explicitly state what the ultimate goal of learning is, but careful examination of the content will often provide evidence of a particular view of the goal.

In the learning of teachers also, there are different ways of thinking about the ultimate goal of all teacher-learning processes, and these different ways of thinking will result in very different ToTing practices (from designing, through planning and implementing to assessing), and it's crucial that we acknowledge this throughout the book.

Before describing different possible goals we want to state that, of course, everything we discuss below presupposes that teachers have a good subject knowledge.

1.1 Possible goals for teacher learning

So what are different ways of thinking about the ultimate goal of teacher learning? We have often asked ToTs and educational planners what they were, ultimately, aiming to 'produce' or achieve. Answers, when these were forthcoming, varied greatly but seem to fall into five main categories. These are to produce:

- 'good teachers'
- people who are 'good' at teaching
- professionals
- reflective practitioners
- technicists

Before we discuss each of these in turn together with their implications for what teachers need to learn, we'll briefly consider the notion of 'good' in the phrases 'good teacher' or 'good teaching'. Again we'll need to return to this when we discuss the practice of assessing teaching (see Part 4), but what we'd like to point out here is that 'good' can look very different in different contexts. This may be because of different ultimate learning goals but it may also be for wider cultural reasons which determine the ultimate goals of education as a whole in any one system. Some education systems, for example, aim primarily at producing citizens to fit into society as it currently exists. At the other extreme, some systems claim to aim more at actualizing the potential of each individual child. Matters are of course rarely quite as 'black and white' as this, and most education systems have ultimate goals which change over time and lie somewhere between these extreme positions. Culturally specific views of education as a whole influence which of the ultimate goals for teacher learning is likely to be most prevalent as well as what exactly is considered as 'good'. A system whose primary aim is to 'produce citizens' might for example favour a technicist goal for teacher learning, where a teacher might be considered to be 'good' if they are doing more or less exactly the same as others. On the other hand a system claiming to actualize the potential of every child is more likely to choose, for example, a reflective practitioner goal for teacher learning, and notions of 'good' will include the ability to demonstrate unique and context-appropriate behaviour.

We now look at each of these goals in turn, and consider some ways they will influence the planning and teaching of programmes for teachers of whatever kind.

Goal 1 Producing 'good teachers'

The focus here is on people and their developing identity as a 'teacher'. The goal here emphasizes 'turning' a person into a teacher. From the point of view of the person hoping to become a 'good teacher' through initial teacher preparation programmes a major focus in the initial stages of their teacher learning is on developing sufficient belief and confidence to feel enough like a teacher to be able to survive in classrooms. This feeling of being, or being like, a teacher grows as a result of more or less successful attempts at seeming to be a teacher and being accepted as such in a given context. What this actually looks like in any one society will vary according to often long-standing and taken for granted norms regarding the role of the teacher. On initial teacher preparation courses, people will also vary in how much they feel this process of looking and behaving like a teacher in their context requires them to change themselves. Some may feel that this requires a complete change of identity, while others arrive already believing they have certain 'teacherly qualities'. Subsequently, whether in initial teacher preparation or later, the focus of learning can expand from preoccupation with themselves and their identities as teachers to a focus on pupil behaviour during lessons and finally a concern with pupil learning and developing a range of relationships that will enable each pupil to learn.

If you ask people (who all have vast experience as pupils) about good teachers they will mention a range of qualities such as being knowledgeable, kind, patient or even attractive. When non-teachers talk about good teachers the focus is on the personal and interpersonal qualities and skills that good teachers seem to have, and it is a teacher's ability to form these relationships that is being referred to when non-teachers describe 'good teachers' in terms of the qualities mentioned above. Non-teachers therefore tend to talk about the personal side of being a teacher rather than any explicit reference to 'learning' as such. It is, however, important to remember that people only feel good about teachers who, in addition to establishing such relationships, value their efforts, understand their needs and difficulties, and enable them to be, and feel that they are, successful learners.

Implications for ToTing include the need to:

- pay attention to the emotions of the learner, particularly with respect to confidence building
- identify what potentials each person has in terms of 'teacherly qualities' and personal skills and work with and from these
- address areas such as interpersonal skills, conflict resolution
- consider using drama techniques (focusing, for example, on body language and voice use) to support the personal public presentation aspects of the work

Goal 2 Producing/developing 'good teaching'

The focus here is on the activity and how it is carried out rather than the individual. Some people have seen teaching as a craft, and in the sense that all of us have learned from more experienced others, at the least through our experience as pupils, it can be seen as such. Others have tried to see it as a science and think this involves identifying a single best method that might be universally applicable through more or less 'scientific' research and experimentation. However, as those working in teacher education have become more aware of the complexity and influence of context, current thinking acknowledges that there can be no 'one best way' (just think of your own teaching – what works in one class may not in another). Although the search for the one best method has not therefore been successful, research is increasingly discovering ways of thinking (rather than particular ways of teaching) that may be appropriate across a range of contexts.

In addition, we recognize that in the activity of teaching many things are happening simultaneously, and for each there is more than one way of doing it: teaching has therefore been called a complex, open skill. The complexity refers to the fact that any period of teaching may involve a range of activities. It may involve the teacher in talking, looking, listening and moving, and within these it might be talking to explain, talking to give instructions, talking to provide a model, listening to know what to say next, to assess and evaluate, to understand, looking to maintain discipline, to see if students are on task, moving to see what students are doing, to emphasize what is being said, or to demonstrate. A teacher's in-class teaching activity may also involve reading and writing: for example, reading what students have written, reading the textbook, reading what you've written on the board and writing on the board and in notebooks and, again, teachers have different reasons for doing this reading and writing. In addition, this is only one side of the story, since the pupils will also be engaged in a whole range of activities that interact with those of the teacher. This multiplicity of simultaneous activity is one of the things that makes the activity of teaching *complex.*

The fact that for each reason for a teacher doing something (e.g. talking) there are many ways of doing it at any given point in any particular classroom (some of which are likely to be more appropriate for the pupils' learning than others) makes this an *open* skill. For example, possible reasons for talking include: to explain, to present, to model, to chat, to question, to support, to comment, to motivate, to have fun and to manage behaviour. If we take the last of these reasons, possible ways for managing behaviour through talk include: withdrawing talk (being silent), shouting, whispering, using a mocking/sarcastic tone of voice and simply saying something. And the kinds of things that could be 'said' include: 'look X is behaving nicely', 'shut up', 'if you don't behave, I'll ... ', 'well done! Here's a sticker', 'please be quiet, I want to ... ', 'that's your first warning', 'I feel sad when I hear you ... ', 'when you do that, X can't ... '. The choices that the teacher makes, often with no time for conscious decision-making, depend on their judgement of the immediate situation as well as their beliefs.

Which of the above can you imagine yourself saying? Which would you never say? What else might *you* say to manage pupil behaviour through talk?

As you read the list of things that a teacher could choose to say to manage behaviour, we expect there were some you could imagine yourself saying and others you couldn't. Your feelings reflect your beliefs on a range of issues that are rarely openly discussed, such as the nature of human beings (essentially 'good' versus essentially 'naughty'), or the exercise of power (used in one's own interests or in the interests of others). Your responses to the above may also reflect your past experience and the behaviour management policies (whether explicitly stated or not) in the institutional cultures you have worked in.

In contrast, a *closed* skill is when there is only one right or currently accepted 'best' way of doing something, for example building a brick wall, or taking an X-ray. Teaching, on the other hand, requires great personal creativity and flexibility and some would say it amounts to professional artistry. Teaching therefore can be said to contain elements of an art, a craft and a science.

Some implications for the conditions that ToTs need to provide arising from these various views of teaching are:

Teaching as an art

- a safe context and opportunities to make personal choices and experiment with novel ways of doing things

Teaching as a craft

- access to experienced others

Teaching as a science

- access to the latest scholarly thinking and research

Teaching as a complex open skill

- opportunities for learners to practise and receive comments on the component parts of skill in a safe environment
- opportunities for learners to practise putting the parts together, and managing the complexity in real-world situations, and be supported in doing so.

Goal 3 Producing teaching professionals

By professional here we do not simply mean a manner of being (which in our part of the world often seems to involve concealing emotions, wearing a particular style of clothing, or acting in a distant and efficient manner). We do, though, understand that looking like, and therefore being accepted as whatever the contextually accepted model of 'a teacher' is considered to be may be very important for the beginner learner, in aiding them to develop a sense of teacher identity (see discussion on 'good teacher' above). Here we consider some features of what professions such as architects, doctors and lawyers have in common, in order to get a sense of what professionalism might mean. Such professionals have high social status; they are well-paid and accountable to their clients; they belong to a professional body; they have had a considerable period of professionally focused education beyond their first degree in preparation for their role and they, as a matter of course, keep themselves up-to-date with developments in their field, through reading and contributing to professional journals or debates. Professionals are autonomous and use relevant knowledge and skills to make practical decisions in a range of ever-changing situations. If a system hopes to produce professional teachers, then it will need to consider the relevance of the above issues in programme development.

Implications of trying to produce professional teachers include the need for teachers to:

- understand how and to whom they are accountable
- be able to obtain recognized specialist qualifications as a result of a considerable period of study
- see the value of, and have easy access to, professional journals
- participate in professional debates
- belong to and participate in the activities of a professional body (such as reading newsletters, attending conferences)
- develop flexible, informed decision-making skills

Goal 4 Teachers as reflective practitioners

The term 'reflective practice' has been a 'buzzword' in teacher education since the 1980s. It emerged initially from Schön's studies (1983, 1987) of the qualities and behaviours that characterized good professionals. This observed that a lot of the behaviour involved in professional practice was based on complex ways of thinking before, during and after the visible professional practice.

At about the same time as Schön's work, research began to identify what good teachers did in the classroom. ToTs working then believed that this research provided the basis for a clear syllabus on which to base their teaching. But, getting learners to replicate the behaviours of good teachers didn't produce the expected results. It became clear to many ToTs that, although their learners might be able to practise these behaviours, they did not have the same effect on pupils and their learning as had been reported by researchers' studies of 'good teachers'. One of us remembers a learner, at that time, dutifully 'waiting' before eliciting an answer from pupils (as instructed, based on 'wait-time' research and 'what good teachers do'), but waiting impatiently, looking at her watch to count off the required number of seconds. This, of course, did not have the desired effect that a good teacher's 'waiting' with belief that more pupils could work out the answer might have had. The learner had used the strategy without understanding why. The seeming failure of using the outcomes of 'good teacher behaviour' research as a set of behaviours for all learners to imitate, showed there was more to good teaching than executing a set of prescribed strategies. What mattered as much or even more than what the teachers were actually doing, was their understanding of why (and where and when) they were doing it; in other words how they were thinking before, during and after teaching in real classrooms. In part this relates to appropriate planning and selection of strategies to use, but also to a teacher's understanding while actually using them. So, ToTs turned to ideas from Schön's work (and by now the work of many others in fields such as teacher thinking, and teacher cognition) to help them consider how best to focus on teacher thinking as well as and in relation to behaviour on their programmes. Some of what this implies particularly for overall programme design is illustrated in Part 2.

The conclusions drawn from these two strands of work (the study of professionals, and disappointing attempts to get learners to replicate the behaviours of good teachers) seemed to coincide in their appreciation of the importance of the *thinking* behind behaviour, and so the notion of the reflective practitioner became perhaps the most written about in teacher education literature during the late twentieth century. However, as with many terms, it has come to mean different things to different people. It has been talked about with respect to:

- what is thought about
- how deeply it is thought about
- the relationship between what is thought about and what actually happens
- how other people's thinking and experience is integrated into this personal thinking process
- strategies and tools which support the thinking

Later in this and subsequent Parts we will suggest processes which might help make sense of the notion of reflection, as well as help learners, and ToTs, become more reflective in, for and about their practice. We do not go into this in detail here as it would be too big a 'diversion' from the discussion of goals and their implications. However, we do suggest you might like to refer back to these implications after you have read about the 'pendulum' in Chapter 3 and noticing and observing in Chapter 12.

The main implications for ToTing involve the need to address learners' knowledge and skills in the following areas:

- noticing and observing what is actually happening in classrooms
- what teachers think about (i.e. themselves, learning, exams, the influence of the wider context) and why
- how teachers use what they think about in relation to their teaching, their pupils, their colleagues
- when teachers give themselves time and space to think – immediately after teaching, sometime later, on the bus, in the bath
- how teachers (can) access and use other people's ideas in their thinking

Goal 5 Technicists

A technicist is someone who executes someone else's plans, and there is a view of teachers that sees this as their role. In the same way that a builder needs to follow an architect's plans to the last detail if the building is to be safe, sturdy and exactly as the architect envisaged it, so a teacher needs to follow syllabuses and course plans equally closely if the outcomes expected by the designers are to be achieved. The builder needs to have certain skills and use the materials the architect has specified in order to be able to execute the architect's plans. So a technicist teacher also needs to use personal skills and the materials provided.

We consider complete fulfilment of this goal to be ultimately impossible because in teaching, unlike building a house, there are many other important *people* more or less directly involved, namely the pupils, their parents and educational managers. In addition, as we have said above, it is not just what a teacher does and how they do it that matters but also their own reason for doing them. In other words if a teacher does something simply because they are expected to (a common state of affairs for many teachers in technicist systems), they are likely to do it in a very different and probably less effective way from another teacher who may have chosen to do the same thing because they believe it will, at that moment and in that context, help the learning of their pupils.

However, we recognize that both education systems and individual beginner teachers may consider this goal to be desirable in the short to medium term. Systems may aim for a technicist teacher workforce because they are poor in human and material resources, and/or indeed they see technicist teachers able to follow syllabuses and materials consistently as a way of 'limiting the damage' which teachers with insufficient subject knowledge and/or training might inflict on learners. In addition, beginner teachers' early concerns, as we have seen, centre around survival in the classroom and so they often appreciate a certain amount of being told what to do because they find being able to execute a very structured set of procedures confidence-boosting and supportive in the early stages of their career.

In sum, we see this goal for teacher learning as being, at best, a possible stepping stone for both individuals and systems towards the more complex goals represented by various combinations of the other goals discussed above. Unfortunately, in our opinion, at present there is a movement among policy makers even in some resource-rich systems, towards behaving as if this goal should be the sole one, deriving perhaps from a misplaced notion of what accountability for teachers should involve, namely that there is a 'best practice' that everyone should be following and that can be objectively assessed through observation of teacher behaviour (and pupils' exam results). If you look back at our discussion of reflective practice above, it is clear that 'good teaching' is not just a matter of displaying a certain set of behaviours, since in any case perceptions of 'correct behaviours' change as new theories of learning emerge.

Implications of trying to produce technicist teachers include the need for learners to:

- share the syllabus and materials designers' ways of thinking
- develop the skills to carry out the requisite in-class operations and activities that these ways of thinking engender, in ways that are consistent with the expected outcomes

1.2 A very quick look at ideas about teacher learning

There are currently a number of different perspectives on teacher learning. Before we go any further we would like to take a quick look at some of these as they relate to the different goals above, since they are inevitably closely connected. For example, if you found yourself drawn to a particular goal above you might like to think about whether and to what extent it corresponds to your, perhaps implicitly held, view of how teachers learn. Views of teacher learning underlying a particular chosen ultimate goal will also, of course, affect design and subsequent decisions in the ToTing process (see Chapter 4).

Naive views of the 'good teacher' would say that good teachers are born and not made, and that therefore one has to be the 'right' kind of person to be a teacher, and that, if it needs to occur at all, teacher learning, assuming appropriate selection of learners, will happen more or less automatically on the job. More recent views of teacher learning see identity and (inter)personal skills development as integral components of planned processes for teacher preparation. Socio-cultural perspectives see teacher learning as coming about through increasing degrees of participation in and membership of a culture of teachers in a given context. This perspective relates to both the goal of 'being a good teacher' (in 'identity' terms) and also that of becoming a professional in the sense of 'joining the club' of teachers. There are also cognitive views of teacher learning, with (social) constructivism being the most common. Such views emphasize the importance of engaging the learner in personal meaning-making and, in social constructivism, the important role that interaction with others plays in the process is again highlighted. Constructivist views relate to the goal of the reflective practitioner and the focus on the thinking and concepts that lie behind the action. Finally, there is also skill theory which sees 'intelligent action' as being developed through cyclical processes of supported trial and error and which relates to the goal of 'good teaching'. As for the technicist goal, this seems to suggest a now outdated allegiance to a behaviourist view of learning.

If you are now wondering 'help, what should *I* be thinking?', one way of approaching the quandary is to look at the most recent ideas. Chronologically these theories of teacher learning go from behaviourist to skill theory and constructivism and on to socio-cultural views, but as we will see in the story that follows you need to be careful not to feel that you must choose one theory and ignore all the others.

1.3 A story

Before we go on to consider what teachers need to know, let's have a change of style. Below is a version of a traditional Asian story that we often tell on courses for teachers and use in many ways.

Story 3

Six blind men used to meet up once a week to chat in the coffee shop. One day when they were talking, the conversation turned to elephants, and they each realized that they didn't really have a clear idea about this animal called 'elephant' at all. They all agreed that before they next met they would find a way to go to 'see' an elephant. They knew that there were elephants at the zoo/the circus that had just come to town/the elephant orphanage {select as contextually appropriate!}, and over the next week each man went to 'see' an elephant.

The first blind man, on reaching the elephant, stretched out his hand and touched the huge body of the elephant. 'Gracious!' he thought, 'So, elephant is like a big wall! Well, well, who'd have thought it!' The second blind man stretched out his hand and found the elephant's trunk, and he thought, 'hmm, long and wriggly, like a snake!' The third man found a leg of the elephant and thought to himself how like a tree trunk an elephant was. The fourth touched the elephant's ear and it reminded him of a big fan, the fifth found a tusk and decided that elephant resembled a spear – long and hard and pointed at the end – and the sixth found the tail that, he thought, was like a rope.

At their usual time, they all gathered again at the coffee shop, and all agreed that it was good they now had a clear idea of what kind of animal an elephant was. 'Strange though', said one, 'I hadn't thought an elephant would be like a spear.' 'Spear', said another, 'don't be silly, it's much more like a snake.' 'A snake!' said a third amazed, 'What do you mean a snake, of course it isn't, it's like a wall.' 'Wall?' said a fourth, 'I think you must be a bit mad, I'd have said it was like a rope' . . . and as they listened to each others' ideas they became more and more irritated, because they all had touched the elephant, they each knew what it was like, their experience had told them so. So they argued and argued and argued . . . and the sad thing is that, if they had all tried to see how each one of them was actually partially right (and not completely wrong), and so had put all their ideas together, they would all have had a better understanding of what an elephant is in fact like.

> Before reading on, take a moment to consider why you think we have told this story at this point . . .

We thought we'd include it now for several reasons. The most important for this discussion is that we are not offering these goals, or broad views of teacher learning as a menu from which you should choose just one. There is probably some truth in all ways of considering them both. In practice ToTs may want to find a way of expressing their own view of the ultimate goal and broad understanding of teacher learning by combining some or all of the different perspectives when developing their own vision of the teacher learning that they are trying to support.

Other reasons include:

- to provide a 'bit of light relief' – and a different mode of mind use (see Chapter 2)
- to remind us all that in the complex, open business of teaching and ToTing there can be no one 'right way/answer' – remember that we too can only have a limited perspective on the elephant as a result of our own experiences even though we have tried to go round it, and study it and access other peoples' experiences to get as clear a picture as we can
- to highlight the value of teacher collaboration
- the final reason we told this story (and tell others in this book) has to do with the role of stories in teacher knowledge and learning, which we will discuss further in Part 3

NB how we had several different reasons for telling you this story. You will find that many of the activities that ToTs use, particularly with groups of learners, have this multi-purpose role. In practice you will not necessarily highlight all the purposes with your course participants, but you need to be aware of them to manage the particular learning process effectively. In addition, being aware of all of them is useful since we have found that, the more we are aware of all the different purposes that a particular activity can fulfil, the more usable the activity is in different contexts, albeit with different emphases. For example, if you think about the 'blind men and the elephant' we have used it in other contexts as a conflict-resolution technique when people have seemed reluctant to acknowledge the validity of each others' opinions or perspectives, or as a way of introducing the importance and usefulness of small group work.

> We mentioned before the above aside that you would need to develop your own vision of the ultimate goal of teacher learning. By vision we do not necessarily mean exactly what you think it is feasible to achieve in the immediate term, but something that gives you direction and so, crucially (as we will see in Chapter 2), guides not only what you do but how you do it. It matters how you as ToTs think, just as it matters how teachers think (see Story 2 above).

Creating a clear vision of your own direction is important for a further reason. Whereas policy makers, curriculum designers and coursebook writers may impose their vision on classroom teachers, this is far less often the case for ToTs.

1.4 What 'good' teachers know

As we have seen above, different goals of teacher learning imply different things that teachers need to know or know how to do and therefore learn. As another way of looking at what teachers need to learn, we turn now to the insights gained from recent studies in teacher knowledge and teacher thinking/cognition, which have begun to explore and try to describe what it is that recognized 'good' teachers actually do know. So another way of thinking about the goal of teacher learning is to look at teachers in your own context who are already what it is you want your learners to become (i.e. who you consider to be 'good') and discover what knowledge they are drawing on in their work.

Researchers have written about teacher knowledge in many ways. We are going to suggest two ways of looking at teacher knowledge that we have found useful. The first way is to classify the detail of teacher knowledge in terms of what it is they need to know, and the second is to group teacher knowledge in terms of what knowledge they use and how they have come to know it. In this Part you (the reader) may find that we stretch your definition of the word' knowledge' to cover more than is often understood by the term 'know'.

> As an exercise you might like to think (or even make a note of) what you mean when you say that somebody knows something.

1.4.1 The content of teacher knowledge

The first and most conventional way of thinking about teacher knowledge is to make lists and group the topic areas that teachers are thought to need to be knowledgeable about. There are many such lists. One of the best known is one devised by Shulman (1987) which sees the most important knowledges as being

- content knowledge – knowledge of the subject that you are teaching
- general pedagogical knowledge – classroom management and assessment techniques

- curriculum knowledge – knowing what is in the curriculum, understanding why it is there and planning how to 'cover' it within the time available
- pedagogical content knowledge – knowing the techniques that are available to use for teaching your subject
- knowledge of learners and their characteristics – your learners in general and the individuals making up a particular class
- knowledge of the educational context – the education system as a whole and the school in particular
- knowledge of educational ends, purposes and values and their philosophical and historical backgrounds – the ultimate goals of education within the society and what education is thought to be for

Although by 'subject' Shulman (1987) meant the subjects of the school curriculum, a ToT's 'subject' is teaching/being a teacher in a specific context. In other words, for example, while both ToTs and their learners need to develop similar 'general pedagogical knowledge', they will differ in what it is they need to learn under 'content knowledge' and 'pedagogical content knowledge'. For you as ToTs we hope this book addresses most of these either directly or through suggesting strategies for getting the knowledge when it is context-specific.

A problem with a broad teacher learning curriculum outline such as Shulman's is that it tends to be interpreted as being 'this is what people need to be told about', and perhaps also 'this is what people need to practise doing' (in terms of pedagogic techniques). This view does not, though, help us to see that there are big differences in how the various aspects of knowledge are learnt. For example, while knowing about how the education system works as a whole may require only a few hours' study, pedagogical knowledge will need a great deal longer to develop.

1.4.2 Types of teacher knowledge

As ToTs we find it more helpful to think of, and group, teacher knowledge in terms of how different types of knowledge are learned. By 'learned' here we are not talking about the overarching macro theories about how teachers learn, whether through formally designed programmes or not (e.g. socio-cultural approaches to teacher learning discussed above), but rather about the micro-processes involved in how people come to learn the specific things we want them to know, in for example a specific session or series of sessions, as part of a particular programme. We have said we find it more helpful to talk about different types of knowledge and, put simply, there seem to be three kinds of knowledge that teachers need. These are: knowing about things, knowing how to do things and knowing to use appropriate aspects of the other kinds of knowledge while actually teaching. We'll expand a little further on these types of knowledge below.

Knowing about (KA)

What teachers know about and use in their thinking includes:

- their subject, the aims and role of the subject within the wider curriculum
- how the subject is learnt, the existence of strategies to support learning
- the school and its policies, accepted norms and procedures within the education system
- the students, their backgrounds, their needs
- strategies for managing their own ongoing professional learning, the existence of professional organizations and support networks, and journals in their subject area

Knowing how (KH)

The expertise of teachers includes being able to:

- use strategies to support pupils and their own learning
- notice important features of classrooms and organizations
- promote conditions which support the learning processes
- assess learning
- relate to students, other professionals, parents and colleagues
- fulfil other professional obligations
- access and use new ideas and/or theories to think, plan and/or assess

Knowing to (KT)

The expertise developed over time by 'good' teachers allows them to:

intuitively and instantaneously use what they know (whether it is a knowing about or knowing how type of knowledge) at just the right moment, and in just the right way to support the learning of their particular learners, in their classroom.

1.4.3 Types of knowledge and goals of teacher learning

How does all this discussion about the aspects/types of knowledge that teachers use relate to 1.1 above in which we thought about the possible goals of teacher learning? Let's illustrate the connections by taking some of the implications that we drew out under each goal in 1.1 above, and trying to identify the types of knowledge that they involve.

Previously we have suggested that implications of the various goals included:

(a) for 'producing good teachers' – a need to focus on areas like interpersonal skills, conflict resolution and the use of drama techniques
(b) for 'developing good teaching', and viewing teaching as a complex open

skill – the ability to make appropriate choices to act or to respond to others' action, at the appropriate time

(c) for producing 'teaching professionals' – a need for easy access to professional journals

(d) for producing 'reflective practitioners – a need for teachers to understand what they think about and why they think about some topics and not others

(e) for producing 'technicist' teachers – teachers who can interpret syllabus and course materials in the manner that the designers intended (although we have already argued that this never likely to be completely feasible given the nature of individuals and their contexts)

Before we say what we think, you might like to spend a moment considering what kind of knowing (KA, KH or KT) you think is principally involved in each of the above implications.

For each of the implications above, our thoughts about the type of knowledge involved (following the lettering above) are:

(a) As you have probably recognized we see a need to focus on areas like interpersonal skills, for example, as mostly to do with 'knowing how', and then later 'knowing to'.

(b) We see the ability to make appropriate choices to act or to respond to others' action, at the appropriate time, as *the* example requiring 'knowing to' and as the core of the knowledge that teachers need to acquire. We say this since in-classroom teaching is the principal activity of teachers. As we will discuss later this 'knowing to' development relies on specific 'knowing how,' skills, those of noticing, thinking and learning from experience (some might call all of this 'reflecting').

(c) The ability to access professional journals is an example of 'knowing about' in the sense of knowing they exist, where to find them and knowing what is in them, and of 'knowing how' in terms of reading and language as well as how to use what is in them.

(d) Teachers who understand what they think about and why they think about some topics and not others will have come to know themselves, and the process of doing so will have contributed to the development of 'knowing to'. If you become aware of what you do and do not notice (and so think about), it can help you to notice more or differently in the action of teaching, and so be able to be more responsive.

(e) To be able to interpret syllabus and course materials in the manner that the designers intended, teachers need to 'know about' various ways of designing syllabuses and the thinking behind these different ways, as well as 'knowing how' to use this knowledge to analyse and understand their own syllabus and plan accordingly for their own circumstances.

Why is it important to make these connections? As you will see in the next chapter the different kinds of knowledge are learned in different ways and so ToTs need to know what kinds of knowledge are going to be needed (according to the ultimate goal/vision) in order to be able to design and plan programmes and sessions that will provide appropriate learning opportunities.

Now that we have explained the difference between KA, KH and KT you will understand that as ToTs you too have new knowledge of all three types to learn. For example, while all the implications of the goals discussed above have relevance to the learner teachers that ToTs teach, some of them will be relevant to ToTs themselves. Let's look at the implication of *needing to pay attention to the emotions of the learner teacher in terms of confidence building* from the goal of 'producing good teachers'. This suggests that ToTs need to develop their own 'knowing to' expertise in terms of noticing and accurately interpreting indications of emotional states in their learners. ToTs need such expertise to be able to react in a way that will encourage teachers to go on making the most of the available opportunities for learning.

Through this book we can only support your 'knowing about'. Ultimately it will be up to you to develop the other forms of knowing, as well as increasing your 'knowing about' through further reading. We suggest further reading, including journals you might want to keep an eye on and, in Part 3, we also suggest strategies you might try out, to help yourselves to develop appropriate 'knowing how' and 'knowing to' expertise in the teaching of teachers.

If in reading the above you thought about what you mean by the term 'know', you might like to look back at what you wrote and consider it again in the light of what you have just read. We hope you will see that what we mean by 'know' is not just what teachers can talk about (the more traditional understanding of 'know'), but also what, more or less consciously, drives what they actually do.

The next chapter discusses the conditions needed for the three different kinds of knowledge to be learned.

Chapter 2

How teachers learn

In 1.2 above we mentioned various broad perspectives on how teachers do learn, whether guided and supported to do so or not. In this chapter we are considering teacher learning on planned programmes designed to support that learning. In general terms in planned programmes for teacher learning there has been a shift away from a theory–application approach (here is the theory – now go and apply it) for one main reason – it doesn't work and has given rise to many 'moans' from both ToTs and their learners about a perceived 'theory–practice' gap! The approach ignores both the teacher as a person and the context in which s/he is/or will be working, and so is bound to be less than effective. Current approaches might be labelled 'investigation–articulation', where the learners' experiences and the beliefs and concerns to which they give rise are investigated and a professional language of teaching drawn from relevant conceptual tools (theories) is developed to talk and think about these experiences, and to plan for future teaching which will be more supportive of pupil learning.

Teacher Learning syllabuses may be based on different ultimate goals ('good' teacher, 'good' teaching, professionals, reflective practitioners, technicists or some combination of these) in different contexts. Nonetheless all three types of knowledge discussed in 1.4 above will need to be developed. We will therefore go into more detail here about how people come to have these different types of knowledge, i.e. how they learn them. By 'learn' we here mean something broader and deeper than just having been told it (as in the old theory–application approach). We expect that like us you can remember (or know you have forgotten) many things you were once told, and perhaps were even successfully examined on, that as far as you can judge have not actually made any difference to what you now believe or how you now behave.

2.1 Knowing about (KA)

Consider some of the things you know about, some of the information you know that you could easily tell us. We are thinking of things such as: your own address;

home telephone number if you have one; some of the rhymes or stories you were told as a child; the best route to take from home to work at different times of the day; where to get a tyre on your car or bicycle mended or, less personally, what makes rain fall, which planet is furthest from the sun or what has been reported in the news today. For whatever you know, why do you know it and how did you come to know it? For much of it, you know it either because somebody told you, or you read it. But of all the things that people tell you and you read, the ones you retain and use are ones that you see as being personally relevant either because you need them for daily life or because they are interesting to *you*. (One of us has to keep asking 'which planet is it that's furthest from the sun?' each time we reread the section above! Although this information is not particularly relevant to either of us, and neither of us need to know it for any daily practical purpose, it interests one of us, but not the questioner above!)

Another aspect of KA relates to concept development. We will try and show what we mean by taking an example from medicine. For most people the concept of 'dressing a wound' means, for example, cleaning a cut and sticking on a plaster. However, for professional wound dressers (doctors, nurses) the concept is much more complex and involves knowing about and identifying different types of wounds, different ointments and different types of dressing material and whether, after cleaning, wounds need to be covered or left open to the air. Similarly many of the words teachers use are very 'everyday' words, for example 'learning' and 'teaching'. While the relatively simple idea behind the use of these words is usually sufficient in daily conversation (although see our discussion of 'teacher' in the General Introduction), practising teachers need a much more complex and professional understanding. For concepts to develop, the starting point for learners will be a recognition that there is more to know, coupled, if the motivation for learning is a practical one, with a feeling that their existing way of thinking is no longer sufficient for their needs. The process of development then requires learners to have access to a variety of alternative ways of thinking, through listening or reading, and then to engage in some kind of mental activity and effort to reconsider their existing concept. (We hope that what you have read so far may be helping some of you to develop your conceptual thinking about teaching, teacher learning and knowing – in addition to helping us establish a shared starting point and language for the rest of the book.)

2.2 Knowing how (KH development)

The development of KH relates to the development of skills. We are not here talking about 'skill' in the behaviourist sense of unthinking patterns of visible behaviour, but in the sense of being able to do something. As discussed in Chapter 1, the skills that are required for teaching (from planning and preparing through to in-class teaching and assessing) need to be very closely connected with appropriate professional thinking. For example, they need to be clearly related to aspects of KA such as knowledge about the subject and how it is learned, as well as to knowledge about the learners, the curriculum and so on.

How do people learn skills? The starting point for almost all skill learning is a period of observing skilled people in action and possibly participating personally at a helper level. This is followed by having a go with support and guidance from a more expert other, thinking about what happened, using any observer comments, learning from both mistakes and things that went well, and having another go ... then having another go ... we talk about the skills learning cycle. We are going to take cooking as an example. Everyone has experience of eating, and enjoying the experience (or not). Most people have experience of more or less consciously watching a parent or adult cooking and perhaps also peeling some vegetables or fetching some implements. As people grow older they might be allowed to participate more while still under adult supervision. They taste what they have cooked and think anything from 'yuk' to 'delicious', and also notice other people's reactions, and next time change what they do and how they do it to try and make it more delicious. This cycle is continued over time with ever less support from others, until they reach a point where they feel that what they do and the way they do it is 'good enough' which is when they stop trying to improve further. This point will of course vary according to context. For example, for a working parent who is the family cook, and who has undemanding family members 'good enough' is likely to come sooner than for a full-time chef at a smart restaurant.

The starting point for good teachers in learning their teaching skills will usually have been observation of the teachers who taught them when they were at school (unless the skills in question are historically new, such as, to take a recent example in many contexts, the use of IT in classrooms). This observation will probably not have been conscious, since as students in school they were more concerned with learning, pleasing the teacher, managing their work and trying to succeed. However, because these experiences of receiving teaching will have covered all their most formative years, they constitute a very powerful model of the visible aspects of teaching. This model whether held as positive or negative has considerable impact on how planned teacher learning processes are experienced, and we will discuss the need to make the model conscious for both learners and ToTs (Chapter 8). Further types of observation of discrete teacherly skills, via purposeful video watching or classroom observation and personal experience of more or less successfully trying things out, may also contribute to continued skills development up to the point when learners too feel their skills are 'good enough'. The point at which they do feel this will depend on the norms of their particular teaching context, and the other demands on their teaching as well as their non-teaching time.

2.3 Knowing to (KT)

This type of knowledge, which itself depends on developing specialized skills (e.g. noticing), brings both of the other two types of knowledge (KA and KH) together and is arguably the most important of the three. There can be little point in knowing about things and knowing how to do things if you cannot actually use this knowledge/these skills in the right place at the right time to support learning. Becoming able to use your knowledge and teaching skills appropriately depends on two things. First, teachers need to be skilled at noticing aspects of classroom events (facial expressions of students, what they are saying, who has finished what when, noise levels in various parts of the room, what students are producing …). Next they need to assess and interpret what they notice in order to make almost instantaneous decisions about what to do next. In making those decisions they will, more or less intuitively, draw on their other types of knowledge as they do what seems most appropriate to keep everybody's learning moving towards the desired learning goals.

This ability to make the more or less accurate interpretations on which to base appropriate strategy selection depends in turn on having a stock of processed personal experiences or teaching stories or cases. These experiences allow teachers more or less intuitively to classify the observed features and take immediate appropriate action.

Let's take an example we often use from everyday life: crossing the road. Most adults even in busy urban environments have enough experience to cross a busy road successfully. To a greater or lesser extent they take the decision to cross the road, decide the speed at which they will do it and the route which they will take intuitively and instantaneously. They do not make conscious mathematical calculations about the speed of oncoming traffic in either direction in order to decide whether it is safe to cross, nor whether they need to run. How do they manage to do this so successfully? Those living in urban settings will have had years of building up experience and more or less consciously 'knowing' the conditions in which it is safe to cross. They have to recognize those conditions and so will have built up mental images of features that may be important to cross safely. Some of you may remember, like us, your parents holding your hands as children and telling you to look right, look left and look right again. One of the useful things about this strategy was that it structured the main noticing orientations needed when crossing a road. Repeated frequently over many years, this strategy helped us to notice the important features that determine when it is safe to cross, amass cases and so build up an instinctive understanding of when it was safe to cross.

Even beginner teachers will respond intuitively to events in their classroom based on their stock of experiences as school pupils. Yet these responses may not always be appropriate or in line with how they have been taught to teach. However, as teachers learn to notice more and become more experienced they will become more able to respond more appropriately to a wider range of events in their classroom and use what they have learned about and for teaching since leaving school themselves. What makes them become better able to respond is their increased ability to notice more plus their greater stock of teaching stories based not only on their experience but also on what they have noticed.

For teachers to learn to 'know to', what sorts of learning opportunities do ToTs need to provide? As we have mentioned, teachers need noticing skill development (see Parts 3 and 4) and as much real teaching as possible, together with time to review that teaching and their intuitive actions within it.

We have discussed teacher knowledge in terms of three different types, but in fact these are all integrated within each teacher. We consider ways of supporting this integration at the end of this chapter. First, however, there are certain conditions which are necessary for the development of teacher knowledge and we discuss these next.

2.4 Conditions for teacher learning

Given all the above, we hope it is clear that, whatever your vision of the ultimate goal of ToTing may be, certain conditions are needed for effective teacher learning of all the kinds of knowledge to occur. We discuss these conditions under three main headings: resources and time, psycho-socio affective conditions and, in Chapter 3, planning for integration.

2.4.1 Resources and time

These are the most tangible and are most affected by financial considerations. Ideally we think that the more resources in terms of books, journals, spaces to work, access to people, technology and time the better. None of us do actually work in ideal circumstances, so at a minimum, if all three kinds of knowledge are to be developed, we would suggest the following:

- access to some books about teaching and to relevant educational journals
- adequate space; if working with groups a flat space with movable furniture for working with the whole group and to allow subgroups to work easily. If working one-to-one in schools, a private space
- a blackboard, a flipchart, or brown paper on a wall with pens
- as much time as possible, possibly spaced out over time, in recognition of the fact that skills (especially complex open skills) take time to develop and need to be established in a consistent and coherent manner over time. If you only have a limited amount of time you need to think what it is feasible to accomplish in that time. We discuss this further in Chapter 4
- Access to people of certain kinds. The most essential people that teachers need access to during their learning are pupils. They also need access to their peers and to more experienced colleagues. The presence of one or more ToTs capable of working with groups of teachers and/or individual teachers in their own classrooms and who are as knowledgeable and skilful as possible is also desirable in most contexts (see Part 3)

2.4.2 Psycho-socio affective conditions

We will look at this aspect through the filter of Glasser's Basic Human Needs (1998), because we find this framework for thinking one of the more useful 'conceptual tools' from the humanistic perspective that we have come across.

Even assuming that teachers can see that the content of a programme is relevant, they, just like anybody else, may need motivating, since unmotivated teachers are unlikely to learn. One way of thinking about this, which we have found useful, is to consider how ToTs can make their work help teachers meet their basic psychological needs. These are, according to Glasser: security; a sense of belonging; the need for success; fun and opportunities to make choices. If ToTs can ensure that in sessions or programmes there are opportunities for teachers to experience all of these, then ToTs are more likely to have created conditions that motivate teachers to remain engaged with the learning. In addition, each of these aspects has a specific role to play in teacher knowledge development and teacher learning. You will see that many of the suggested activities later in the book have the establishment or maintenance of these conditions as one of their main purposes. We look at each of these below.

Security

In some parts of the world security continues to mean physical security. In such cases there is little ToTs can do except try to hold programmes or workshops in places that are as physically safe as possible. In most cases when thinking about meeting this basic need we will be referring to psychological security.

In developing 'knowing how' as well as 'knowing to', teachers need time to try things out. Learners will initially inevitably get it 'wrong', make mistakes, be less than perfect. If teachers are going to feel safe enough to take risks and try out new skills, they need to feel that they are in a safe psychological environment. This requires:

- an accepting and non-judgemental attitude
- the building of trust and positive relationships
- everyone in the group (or both people in a pair) knowing about and understanding each others' perspectives and experiences
- a 'blind men and the elephant' acceptance that everyone has valuable perspectives to offer, as long as they are in fact talking about the 'elephant'

Establishing such conditions is a challenge for all of us, not least because our own learning experiences may not have provided us with examples of how to provide psychologically safe environments (see Chapter 8).

A sense of belonging

A second basic human need is that of a sense of belonging. Teachers spend a great deal of time alone with their learners in their classrooms. However, there is a view that sees teacher learning as involving increasing participation in a community of practice. If, for example, your vision includes elements of the goal 'teacher as professional', you will need to make teachers accustomed to seeing themselves as members of a professional community, and possibly of a recognized professional body. One way in which this need for a sense of belonging and the need for cooperation and collegiality as part of teacher professionalism can be satisfied, is by ToTs paying attention to it. Tangible examples of this for us as ToTs are that, when working with a group, we notice and manage the various stages of group life, or when working one-to-one we make sure the teacher learner encounters other members of the professional group to which they will belong. We discuss group dynamics in more detail in Chapter 8 and working one-to-one in Chapters 7 and 10.

Success

Fundamental to all supported learning is the idea that learners should, initially with our help and ultimately without it, be able to do things that they could not do before. It should therefore be a permanent aim of our teaching to ensure that as far as possible our teachers feel at least some success as a result of everything they attempt as they go through the course and leave the course with a sense of achievement. You may wonder how this can be possible (especially during learning), if as we have said above they will inevitably 'make mistakes', and 'get things wrong' as they learn skills. Although they will not be perfect, they will hopefully have successfully achieved some of what they set out to do, even if it is simply having had the courage to try something new for them. It is the ToT's responsibility to recognize the successes achieved (see Part 3) and help the learners to recognize them too. This need to celebrate success can easily be overlooked, as ToTs may be more concerned with assessing learners' 'failures' in order to guide their planning of future sessions. This highlights the need for ToTs to have (in addition to a positive attitude), sufficiently well-developed noticing skills to be able to notice successes as well as failures and to assess individual learner progress against explicit criteria, and/or show learners how to do this for themselves.

Fun

Teachers have busy lives and a very responsible job. Their opportunities for fun can be very rare. If teachers feel they are having fun with us this may well be motivating. In terms of the development of teacher knowledge (especially 'knowing to') fun is also important. A lot of what teachers think they 'know' about being a teacher has been learned through experience of sitting as learners in classrooms being taught and/or being teachers. Much of this may have rarely (if ever) been consciously thought about. It is a kind of taken for granted, intuitive knowing. Some of the things that ToTs will want to do with their learners will involve concept development work or work to help the learners see the usefulness of new ideas they introduce. In these cases, ToTs first need to discover, and help their learners consciously to discover if necessary, what those concepts, even such central concepts as 'learning' or 'teaching' or 'learning teaching' for example, mean to them. Conditions in which such intuitive knowing can be 'surfaced' (see discussion under modes of mind in Chapter 3) include leisure (another argument for having enough time), metaphor (another argument for the use of stories) and fun.

Choices

For many teachers worldwide working in state systems there may seem to be few choices. However, as we discussed when dealing with the development of complex open skills and when discussing 'knowing to', a central ability that all teachers need is the ability to make informed appropriate decisions before, and during teaching. Therefore by providing opportunities for the learners to make all kinds of choices (about how they will work on a task, who they will work with, what they want to study next, what kind of product they would like to end up with and why), ToTs are supporting the development of this ability, as well as meeting this basic psychological need.

But, you may think teachers are adults, they should be capable of motivating themselves, and taking responsibility for their own learning. True. But if ToTs want their learners to become autonomous they need to take control of managing that process – one of the many paradoxes encountered in education at all levels! Often, in our experience, teachers are on programmes because they have been sent, or because there has been a new reform over which they have had no say. In addition, teachers are frequently underpaid and overworked and may be having to attend the programme in their own time. In these circumstances, however 'adult' the teachers may be, their motivation is unlikely to be high, despite the polite displays of apparent interest they may make for our benefit. We believe therefore that paying attention to basic human needs can help to create supportive conditions for the effort needed for transformative teacher learning – that is learning that has a genuine impact on practice regardless of whether 'observers' are present.

We turn now to thinking about how the different kinds of knowledge relate to each other and become integrated within a teacher learner, and how interactions with others, types and sequencing of experiences, can provide the conditions for this process to occur.

Chapter 3

Teachers learning from their own and others' experience – putting it all together

Introduction

In terms of conditions for teachers learning, the degree to which ToTs provide opportunities for different types of teacher learning will of course make a critical difference. As we mentioned above, for *knowing to* be developed as well as integrated with the other types of knowledge, access to real learners and real experiences of teaching is essential. At the end of this chapter we will discuss models which assume such access. However, we know that for most ToTs, the learners with whom they are working do not have access to real pupils during the time that they are working together, whether this time is half an hour or three years. Therefore we begin the chapter by describing the thinking behind a model that tries to bear this reality in mind, while doing its best to provide opportunities for the development and integration of all three types of knowledge. To get to a usable model it's necessary to picture (albeit perhaps simplistically) what actually happens when teachers do integrate different ways of knowing, that is to say how they learn from their own and others' experiences. The way we are going to suggest here is one which we find to be of practical use (see later Parts of the book) for many of the things that we as ToTs have to do.

In order to explain this picture, and before we present it, we feel we need to tell you the story of how we arrived at it. We have come to this way of thinking through puzzling about how it is that 'good' teachers come to *know to* do things in the effective ways that they do. When we have asked teachers questions like 'how did you know to do that then?' they have given answers like 'I don't know, it just felt right'. We have been struggling to understand where that feeling comes from and how to help others to develop that seemingly 'intuitive sense'. Much research of the kind which has asked teachers how they have learned what they know reports teachers as saying they learn best from experience. So it seems that experience of some kind is a necessary component for teacher learning. Research on thinking and intuition suggests that basically human beings have two ways of thinking and knowing (conscious/deliberative and unconscious/contemplative), and three ways in which they can use their minds. Claxton (1997) calls these ways our minds can work 'modes' of mind and we will go into some detail on each since they are relevant to the development of the model.

3.1 Modes of mind

The first way of thinking we have is a conscious one, which Claxton calls 'd-mode' ('d' stands for deliberative as well as for default as in the default setting on a computer). It is the mode of mind people use when they say, for example, 'let me think about that'. It is a mode of mind that uses rational argument and language to work things out. It is the mode of mind that is 'fed' by ideas that are expressed in language. So it is the mode of mind that everyone uses most in studying. As it uses language, it is used when reading for study purposes and listening to lectures or talks. It is therefore the mode of mind you are using now, and also the one that is most characteristically needed to follow the inputs on many programmes for teachers. When people know something as a result of working in this mode of mind, they know they know it. We hope you will have noticed that there is a strong connection between d-mode and *knowing about.* People who are good at using this mode of mind can usually do well in written exams or assignments, can use language well, know the 'jargon' and are seen by others as being clever.

There is another way of thinking, or using our minds, which is unconscious. It is one in which what Claxton (1997) calls the 'undermind' operates on processing experience of all sorts (memories, feelings, impressions and including experiences of thinking in d-mode). This needs much more time to work than d-mode. It is in the undermind that teachers unconsciously hold the personal models of teaching and learning that have been built up over time through such experiences. Undermind unconscious 'thinking' produces experiential knowing, which is responsible for the feeling in phrases like *'It just felt like the right thing to do at the time'.* It is precisely because the undermind works with experiences, rather than ideas mediated through language, that its contents are not easy for people to talk about. Unlike d-mode, people cannot *decide* to think unconsciously, although they can decide to try to provide the conditions in which this mode of mind can operate. These are: *not* using other modes of mind and allowing contemplative time. People who are good at recognizing and using the products of this kind of thinking are often seen by others as 'wise'.

While both the amassing of the experiences needed for this kind of unconscious thinking and the work at converting them into experiential wordless knowing takes time, the outcomes of such work can spontaneously, and rapidly, emerge into our consciousness. This is how we know we engage in such unconscious thinking in the first place! We expect that like us you have had experiences of waking in the morning with the name you couldn't remember the day before clear in your minds, or the solution to a problem you had been struggling with suddenly popping into your head in the middle of a walk in the country. We said above that much of the content of the undermind is unconscious and not easily talked about, but the fact that the results of the work of this kind of unconscious thinking *can* emerge into consciousness is very important to our work as ToTs. When such insights are made conscious they can be talked about (d-mode) and compared and contrasted with ideas presented by the ToT and/or other course participants. However, this is only possible if certain conditions are met. These are the provision of opportunities for leisure and fun, as well as playful work with fantasy and metaphor. In our experience, the importance of providing these conditions tends not to be recognized in the majority of settings in which teachers are taught. We will refer back to the need to provide these conditions frequently in Parts 2 and 3.

The third mode of mind can be called the 'fast-mind' mode, which is used when people need to act rather than to think. As the name suggests, this mode of mind works very quickly and is used when there is no time to 'think' in a conscious sense, as is the case when you are in the middle of the complex open skill of teaching and need to do many things at the same time. When looking at anybody teaching in a classroom what can be seen is a result of them using their fast-mind mode. The ability to use fast-mind mode for effective action depends on experience in two ways. Firstly, repeated supported experience of performing any teaching action will lead to teachers becoming skilled. This can be seen when teachers make use of automatized teaching skills, to which, due to previous experience (practice) they no longer need to pay conscious attention. Here, we hope that you notice the connection between fast mind and *knowing how*. The second way experience influences action is through the outcomes of the work of unconscious thinking, and the sense that this mode of mind use has made of the accumulated examples and cases of teachers/teaching and learners/learning that teachers have encountered (as pupils, members of society and teachers). When observing unplanned and spontaneous actions by teachers using their fast-mind mode in classrooms, what is seen is also a reflection of their experiential knowing. So it is the outcomes of unconscious thinking that are the source of the 'gut feelings' that prompt the intuitive, rapid, responsive actions characteristic of *knowing to* displayed in the fast-mind use of the experienced 'good' teacher, as well as the sometimes surprising behaviours of the novice. We say surprising, because, as ToTs, we have been surprised to see learners teaching in ways which were totally contradictory to the ways that we thought they had learnt to use (because they wrote good assignments and performed well during micro-teaching). While there was obviously a 'theory–practice' gap from our perspective, considering the ways our minds affect our actions has helped us realize that from the learner's perspective there was little 'gap' between their experiential knowing and their action.

To summarize, we have two ways of thinking – conscious and unconscious – and three ways of using our mind: two for thinking and one for acting. Teachers' actions in classrooms result from both kinds of thinking. However, the traditional way teachers consciously 'think' – to study, for example – can usually only be used before and after lessons in planning or reviewing. In in-class teaching, since continuous rapid action is needed, the time for conscious thinking and 'working things out' is not available. When a pupil is misbehaving, for example, there is no time to stand and consciously 'think' something like: 'Now then, here is a child doing X. I could use Y approach to behaviour management, in which case I would have to say/do Z. But research has shown that in the long term this is an ineffective approach, so perhaps I'd better adopt approach A ... ' You can imagine the chaos that might ensue! As teachers so often don't have the time to access their conscious knowledge, they have to rely on their 'intuitions', their experiential knowledge to guide their actions.

Somehow then ToTs need to help teachers use their minds in all three modes if they want to help them develop KA, KH and KT. In order to do so, they need to ensure that the conditions necessary for teachers to use their minds in these different ways are provided. For 'd-mode' this is not a problem since 'language-based inputs' (reading and discussing) are usually provided on ToT courses. Providing conditions in which learners can use their fast mind is less easy to organize as it involves engaging in actual teaching or skill practice for teaching (micro-teaching). For the undermind to be able to process experiences learners need time when they are not using the other modes of mind (social events, leisure time). For example, on an intensive residential course, rather than setting homework, we have set 'beach work' in which participants were asked to bring back one thing from a half-hour walk on the beach. The next day when they were asked why they had chosen the item they brought back with them, some really insightful connections were made (metaphorically) with aspects of the course. This understanding of what feeds unconscious thinking and also of its direct connection to our teaching actions has made us even more aware that participants' whole 'experience' of the programme feeds their unconscious thinking, and that is it the messages sent by what we do and how this is experienced rather than what we say that will more easily affect our participants' future teaching. We have also realized that if we want what we say to make a difference too, we somehow need to 'reach the gut and touch the hearts' of our participants.

Our growing understanding of unconscious thinking, what it works on, when it works and the conditions in which it can become conscious, has given us a couple of acronyms to use in our thinking and planning of ToT programmes. The first is UFO (not an unidentified flying object as you might think, but an undermind feeding opportunity!). This reminds us that how our participants *experience* our programme is important and helps us think about how best to select activities or tasks, or how best to behave. In other words we try to ensure that we would be happy to see participants translate anything that they have experienced on the course to their own teaching situation (for example we do not any longer stand up and give hour-long lectures – if we can avoid it – because we would not be happy if we saw them doing this in their classrooms). We also think about how to include USOs (undermind surfacing opportunities) in our sessions and pro-grammes. This involves consciously planning in opportunities for fun (perhaps games) or for fantasy or for metaphorical work, for example through stories or the beach object (above).

As well as enabling us to develop a practically useful model for planning and implementing our work with teachers, these studies have also helped us begin to find answers to questions like: why don't teachers teach like ToTs tell them to? Why do ToTs talk about a theory–practice gap? Why have our efforts to be helpful and give advice to teachers about what they might do often seemed to make so little difference? Where does expert teachers' 'feel-right feeling' come from and how do they get it?

3.2 Towards a pendulum model

We characterize our three modes of mind as relating to head (conscious knowing), heart or gut (experiential unconscious knowing – people often talk about 'gut feelings for intuition – the kind of feeling that leads expert teachers to claim that something unplanned 'felt right' to do) and hand (action). One of us likes pictures, so below is an illustration that we will use to try to explain how we see the relationships and connections between the three.

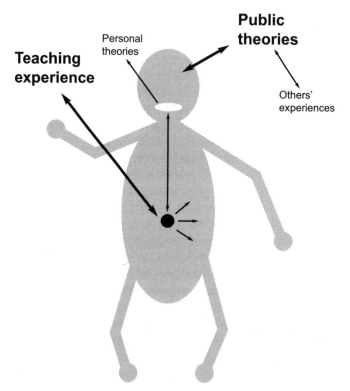

Figure 1   How hand, heart and head can work together

   As we have said, any teacher's experiential knowledge is derived from their life experiences as people, learners and teachers. How teachers make sense of these experiences in turn directly influences the ways they react in subsequent classroom experiences. So there is a thick two-way arrow between the 'heart' and the 'hand'. The descriptions and explanations of experiences that anyone else (fellow participants, authors of relevant texts, ToTs) has been able to put into words we have called 'public Theories' (this book is an example). To be public they have to be in language. They can therefore only interact with teacher's 'heads'. If public theories remain understood purely intellectually they will not affect teachers' action (hand). If they are to influence practice they somehow need to be connected to the 'heart'. The only part of teachers' experiential knowing (heart) with which public theories can demonstrably interact, is any part that has surfaced into their conscious awareness, and which they can therefore put into words (as their personal theories). If public theories can connect with personal theories they can influence learners' 'heart' and so ultimately their 'hand', which is the purpose of any ToT programme. ToTs therefore need to try and help this whole process to happen.

How, though, can ToTs help this to happen in practice? If you look at the picture above it suggests an order of events. A lifetime of experience results in experiential knowing ('heart'), on the basis of which learners' personal theories (articulated or not) are developed. These can emerge into language. If and when they do, public theories can be introduced to interact with/influence any articulated personal theories ('head'). There may then be one of several scenarios two of which we describe here. In the first, the public theories correspond with what learners already think but may not have been able to express very clearly, and so provide them with the professional language to explain and communicate what they already think/know more effectively. This greater clarity will affect practices in which they principally use their head, such as planning, and so potentially enable them to make their previously instinctively 'right' judgements happen more often. In the second, the public theories differ from learners' experiential knowledge in content as well as language. For example, their experiential knowledge or personal theory might say 'elephant is like a fan' while public theory says 'elephant is like a wall'. Here, if learners are willing or able (in terms of having the time and skills/attitudes that will help them do so) public theories may come to influence their personal theories to the extent that learners adapt not only how they talk about them ('head') but also how they feel about them ('heart'), which in turn is likely to affect action ('hand').

We therefore see a movement from hand to heart to head, back to heart and finally back to hand: a five-step process, having only one step with a focus on 'head'(the input of new knowledge about) and two each on 'heart'(for 'knowing to') and 'hand' (knowing how and knowing to). This is a rather different weighting from that on most traditional theory/application programmes for teachers. We see the five-step process as a swinging movement and use the metaphor of a pendulum. The pendulum (see diagram below), gives ToTs a pedagogical model to suggest the sequencing and weighting of the different parts of the programme (twice as much focus on 'hand' and 'heart' as on 'head'). The understanding of ways of thinking and modes of mind also help ToTs decide on what types of event it is appropriate to use when focusing on head, heart or hand. We have found these conceptual tools invaluable in any ToT situation.

We will describe this sequence in simple terms here, but will be elaborating on it, and demonstrating how we use it to make many different kinds of practical decisions throughout the rest of this book.

Here we try to explain the process from the point of view of both the learners and the ToTs.

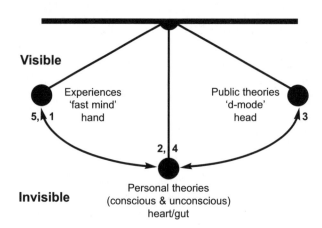

Figure 2   The pendulum: connecting head, heart and hand in ToTing

Step 1

This involves learners in describing an experience. This may be an experience of teaching–learning to be recalled from before the course or be a new experience provided on the course.

ToTs will select the type of experience to use as a starting point according to:

- the type of knowledge (KA, KH, KT) which is the main focus of the learning sequence (the particular 5-step process)
- the main public theory message that they hope participants will remember from the sequence (and that the ToT may need to input at step 3)

Depending on the level of participants' noticing skills, the ToT may need to help the learners notice certain salient features of the experience.

Step 2

This involves learners in interpreting and explaining the experience that they have noticed and described, and saying what it means to them.

ToTs have to devise a format/provide a structure and an immediate purpose for the learners to engage in such activity.

Step 3

The learners at this point listen to/read about other people's different ways of interpreting/explaining the same or similar experiences.

The ToTs need to provide a structure in which the learner teachers can have access to other people's explanations. These may come from other teachers, from reading or from the ToTs themselves.

Step 4

This is often likely to have begun within step 3.

The learners will be comparing and contrasting different explanations/ interpretations and, hopefully more often than not, trying to synthesize rather than reject outright (as the blind men did) any that do not seem to fit. The outcome of this process will vary from one person to another. For some learners this may lead to a genuinely different understanding. For others it will provide confirmation that what they already 'knew' at some level is supported by public theory, and this will be confidence-boosting. For yet others the main benefit of the process so far will have been in finding the language to talk about something that they had not talked about before. There may also be some, particularly those arriving with well-formed and consciously held contrasting ideas, who are tempted to dismiss any consideration of alternative ways of thinking and/or behaving. ToTs will need a range of skills (including listening and interpersonal skills) to coax such learners to consider the alternative views proposed and cope with the confusion that dismantling their established views might bring (see Part 3).

Overall, ToTs have to provide a structure in which this work can be carried out, and elicit and summarize the conclusions from this step.

Step 5

Learners fantasize and try to imagine themselves thinking in their 'new' ways in future teaching situations, considering what the practical implications of this learning might be for their real classroom practice.

The ToT again has to develop a structure for this work to be carried out. Such structures will often involve planning, the development of materials and/or mini demonstrations.

If the learning achieved through such a process is to affect action, ToTs will have to remember the need to plan in UFO and USO opportunities either as part of or outside the 5 step sequence (see Part 2).

As we mentioned many pages ago, all ToT situations take learners away from their real teaching context for at least part of the time. During some programmes learners are never reunited with their teaching context. We find the idea of the pendulum and swinging through the 5 steps of value in planning and implementing the learning carried out away from the teaching context, as we will demonstrate more practically – insofar as one can through words – in the rest of the book.

The development of *knowing to,* complex open skills, and noticing, on which the ability to re-view (see again) and reflect depends, all require or can benefit from access to real teaching contexts. An ideal model for designing teacher-learning programmes would therefore include a sixth step in which what has been imagined at step 5 is actually tried out in their own classrooms. In a programme where the time available is divided into different phases, including one or more phases in school between ToT-supported programme phases, this sixth step is possible. The experience of trying out in classrooms can provide the basis for a variety of new step 1s at the start of new supported learning or study sequences. We see the pendulum movement back into and out of the classroom as allowing for deeper 'swings', which can create even greater momentum for progress.

There are other models in the ToTing, and particularly reflective practice, literature that emphasize the need for participants to spend some phases of a programme in their own classrooms. These are most often expressed in terms of 'cycles'. Such models tend to vary in their number of stages and in how they label each stage. Often their labels are very general, for example Dennison and Kirk's (1990) experiential learning cycle calls the stages 'do' – 'review' – 'learn' – 'apply'. The broad idea of needing to go into and come out of the real classroom world is a useful one and can helpfully inform programme level planning. However, few if any versions of these cycle models have provided us with detailed guidelines about how ToTs can plan provision on programmes which take participants out of their classrooms entirely, or plan at the more detailed level of the session. The existing lack of models for such situations has made us feel that the above 'pendulum', or '5 steps', fills an important gap.

Conclusion

Nothing we've said so far is a prescription, the steps are not *'the'* way to be followed slavishly. They do, though, provide a way of thinking about whole teacher learning (for us and for our learners), and are also a useful tool for checking planning. Programmes are supposedly designed to support teacher learning. Do they in fact provide the kinds of opportunities in the kinds of sequences that are likely to help teachers learn in integrated, relevant, personally meaningful ways? In Part 2 we will see how ToTs can make courses for teachers 'learner-centred' by taking the particular learners' needs and wants into consideration. ToTs also, though, need to remember that courses have to be 'learning' centred, and the '5 steps' suggest two useful maxims that we use (in our thinking and planning) to try to keep the learning of the actual participants central. They are:

- *Begin and end with experience.* This maxim relates to steps 1 and 5. Teachers say they learn *from* experience (Lortie 1975, Hobson 2001) and they are learning *for* future experience. It is the notion of 'relevance' (critical to any teacher learning) (Hobson, Malderez *et al* 2006) that makes it so important to start with experience. Unless learners can see the relevance and connection between what the programme is offering and their own experience, ToTs are likely to be wasting their time. This contrasts with a 'theory application' approach used in typical more conventional TL (teacher learning) programmes, which although it may end with experience (some form of teaching practice during the programme, or simply 'going back' to school), starts with 'theory'. We will look at how this maxim can be helpful in planning and practice in Part 2.
- *'Get out before you put in'.* This means helping learners articulate their own thoughts (*'Get out'*) before telling them whatever it is you want them to

know about (*'put in'*), and relates to steps 2 and 3. This again contrasts with a theory application approach where the ToT begins by saying what s/he has to say and only after this, and only sometimes, provides opportunities for learners to comment. Writing about this maxim reminds us of the meaning of the Latin root of the word 'education': e-ducare – to bring out!

These maxims will be referred to and illustrated time and again throughout the book.

Two further points are worth making here. First, teaching from a theory–application perspective assumes that most of the programme time will be filled by ToT talk, while in contrast, as can be seen from the above, an investigation–articulation approach and the 5-step process, acknowledge that a substantial proportion of course time needs to 'belong to' the teacher participants if they are to be able to articulate and the ToT is to *get out*. Secondly, we do not mean to suggest that all five steps will necessarily be present in any one session of a programme or course. As linguists, we see the parallel between a sentence and the wider text (discourse) of which it is part, and a session and the wider programme/course of which *it* is part. Just as the way in which a sentence is constructed depends on previous and subsequent sentences, as well as its place in the overall structure of the text, so the construction of any individual session will depend on what has gone before, what is to follow and its overall place in the 'whole'. This will be illustrated more fully in Part 2.

The remainder of the book is concerned with how you could use the ideas discussed here in your practices as a ToT. Part 1, through introducing a number of underlying ideas, has begun one of the practices (preparing yourself) that we will be discussing more fully in Part 2, which begins by considering the practices of designing and planning programmes and courses of various kinds.

References

Claxton, G. (1997) *Hare Brain, Tortoise Mind: Why intelligence increases when you think less.* London: Fourth Estate

Dennison, B. and Kirk, R. (1990) *Do review learn apply: a simple guide to experiential learning.* Oxford: Blackwell

Glasser, W. (1998) *Choice theory: a new psychology of personal freedom.* New York: Harper Perennial

Hobson, A. and Malderez, A.,Tracey, L., Giannakaki, M. S., Pell, R. G., Kerr, K., Chambers, G. N., Tomlinson, P. D. and Roper, T . (2006) *Becoming a teacher: Student teacher experiences of initial teacher training in England.* Research Report 744. London: Department for Education and Skills

Hobson, A. J. (2001) Postgraduate history specialists' perspectives on their initial teacher preparation: Preconceptions, experiences and evaluations, unpublished PhD thesis, University of Leeds

Lortie, D. (1975) *School teacher: A sociological study.* Chicago: University of Chicago Press

Schön, D. (1983) *The reflective practitioner: How professionals think in action.* New York: Basic Books

Schön, D. (1987) *Educating the reflective practitioner: Towards a new design for teaching and learning in the professions.* San Francisco: Jossey Bass

Shulman L. S. (1987) Knowledge and teaching: Foundations of the new reform. *Harvard Educational Review* 57(1), 1–22

Tomlinson P. D. (1995) *Understanding mentoring: Reflective strategies for school-based teacher preparation.* Buckingham: Open University Press

Further reading

The transition from being a teacher to being a ToT

Dinkelman, T., Margolis, J., Sikkenga, K. (2006) From teacher to teacher educator: experiences, expectations, and expatriation. *Studying Teacher Education: A journal of self-study of teacher education practices.* 2(1), 5–23

There is, as Cochran-Smith (2003) (Learning and unlearning: The education of teacher educators. *Teaching and Teacher Education* 19, 5–28) has said, little research on what it is that ToTs need to know and how they come to know it. This article (related to teachers in England becoming ToTs at universities) is one of few that we have come across. Our book represents some of what we, in part through our own self study (see journal title above), have come to think it is helpful for teachers becoming ToTs to know.

Goal of teacher learning

We have not found that this topic has been addressed very frequently. In the references that follow usually only one perspective on the ultimate goal is discussed:

Hayes, D. (ed.) (2004) *Trainer development: principles and practice from language teacher training.* Melbourne, Victoria: Language Australia

The trainer in the title here is what we refer to in this book as a ToT. It contains a number of useful perspectives on our work as ToTs drawn from different geographical locations worldwide. There is also a chapter by one of the authors of this volume entitled 'A teacher educator's story of developing understanding', in which the goals of teacher education are discussed.

Hargreaves, A. (2000) Four ages of professionalism and professional learning. *Teachers and Teaching: Theory and Practice* 6(2), 151–82, is an interesting discussion of how perceptions of what teachers have needed to know and be able to do have developed over the past half century together with some of the contextual factors influencing the changes.

Turner, M. and Bash, L. (1999) *Sharing expertise in teacher education.* London: Cassell In Chapter 1 this book offers a discussion of the notion of professionalism and thereafter takes a historical (UK-centred) perspective on ideas about how to support teachers' learning. Chapter 5 provides a useful short bibliography on mentors, mentoring and induction. Included here is a reference to the work of Michael Eraut (1985) Knowledge creation and knowledge use in professional contexts. *Studies in Higher Education* 10(2). This, with the Shulman reference (see above), has influenced the work of many who need to try to understand what it is that teachers know, need to know and how they come to know it.

Bereiter, C. and Scardamalia, M. (1993) *Surpassing ourselves: an inquiry into the nature and implications of expertise.* Chicago and La Salle, IL: Open Court.

This book discusses what is meant by the notion of expertise (progressive problem-solving), why it is desirable and how it may be cultivated. The 'blurb' says:

> Progressive problem-solvers stay healthier, live longer and experience the intense mental pleasure known as 'flow' [see Part 3 References]. They repeatedly go beyond their well-learned procedures, avoid getting into ruts and surpass themselves by reformulating problems at new and more complex levels … They are able to transform insoluble predicaments into soluble problems to the benefit of everyone. Yet many of our present institutions, especially the schools penalize expertise instead of cultivating it.

Our book represents some solutions to some problems that we have arrived at. Our problems may not directly apply to you. However, we hope that our attempt to show the processes through which we arrived at our current solutions will be of relevance. We agree with Bereiter and Scarmadalia that any solution is only temporary and we will continue to need to solve ToT problems for the rest of our careers.

Broad views of teacher learning

We offer three ways to begin to access general ideas about how teachers learn:

Lave, J. and Wenger, E. (1991) *Situated learning: Legitimate peripheral participation.* Cambridge: Cambridge University Press

This is one of the most commonly cited references for socio-cultural approaches to teacher learning.

Richardson, V. (ed.) (1997) *Constructivist teacher education: Building a world of new understandings.* London: Falmer Press

This is one example of a book which subscribes to the personal meaning making or constructivist approach to teacher learning.

Tomlinson (1995) (above) represents the third broad approach to teacher learning, taking in this book a skill theory view of the process.

Finally, we mentioned the current move from the more established theory–application view of teacher education provision to an investigation–articulation perspective. Schön (1987) was one of the earliest writers in this area.

Because this different perspective requires a different pedagogy, a distinct literature is beginning to emerge. For example:

Korthagen, F. A. J. and Kessels, J. (2001) *Linking practice and theory: The pedagogy of realistic teacher education.* London: Lawrence Erlbaum Associates

Loughran, J. (2006) *Developing a pedagogy of teacher education: Understanding teaching and learning about teaching.* Abingdon: Routledge

Loughran, J. and Russell, T. (eds). (1997) *Teaching about teaching: Purpose, passion and pedagogy in teacher education.* London: Falmer

Teacher knowledge

Goodson, I. (2003) *Professional knowledge, professional lives.* Maidenhead: Open University Press

Many of the themes in Part 1 and elsewhere in the book (such as ToTs sharing stories in Chapter 8) are discussed in more depth. He writes, for example, on page 13:

> *the communication and ongoing displacement between theory and practice* [by which we think he means actual in-class teaching, rather than the other practices of ToTing] *is not an intrinsic but rather a socially structured problem. New structures of collaboration ... might help ease the current problems.*

We think what we are proposing here is a new structure for ToTs and learners to collaborate in order to ease the problem of the perceived theory/practice gap.

Carter, K (1990) in a chapter called 'Teachers' knowledge and learning to teach' summarized a lot of the work on teacher knowledge in W. R. Houston (ed), *Handbook of Research on Teacher Education.* New York: Macmillan, 291–310.

In the 1990s the focus turned to trying to understand intuitive and implicit knowing and we would recommend Claxton (1997) as a starting point for pursuing this thread.

Michael Eraut and Peter Tomlinson have also written on implicit knowledge.

Finally, on the issue of the importance of the affective climate to which we return in Parts 2 and 3,

Day, C (2004) *A passion for Teaching.* London: Routledge-Falmer not only summarizes a variety of perspectives on the link between the personal and the professional, but also underlines the need for paying attention to the whole person in our work as ToTs.

Journals

Many journals may be relevant to the topics we discuss in this section, but among the ones to which we frequently refer are:

Studying Teacher Education : A journal of self study of teacher education practices (very recent. First issue 2005). Routledge

Reflective Practice. Routledge

Mentoring and Tutoring. Carfax

Journal of Education for Teaching. Routledge

Teachers and Teaching: Theory and Practice. Routledge

Teaching and Teacher Education. Elsevier

Part 2

Developing Programmes that Support Teacher Learning

Programme development can be seen as an ongoing cyclical process in which the experiences of one programme inform the development of the next. This is true whether or not it is the same programme being revised or a new programme being developed. We see the process of developing *new* programmes to support teacher learning as, initially at least, a more linear-seeming process beginning with fundamental and macro-level decisions and ending with very detailed, concrete, practical decisions about, for example, how to arrange the room for the next session. For convenience we are dividing this process into three stages which are dependent on each other and have a different relationship in time to the actual moment of classroom teaching. The first of these which we call 'Designing' may need to take place a year or more before any actual teaching begins, and will of course be influenced by any previous experiences of the people who are the designers, but for our purposes here we are taking this as the first phase in the process. The second 'Planning' phase can only commence when the designing phase is more or less complete and the 'Preparation' phase in turn depends on plans being clear. It starts in the few days before teaching begins and usually continues during the teaching itself. We now look at each stage in turn.

A word about how all this looks on paper: inevitably what follows is a linear description that tries to unpack and detail elements of a complex process. We hope also we have made the description organized and tidy-looking. Reality, of course, is a lot messier! So, because we have to try to describe this in words in a book, rather than involve you with us as we do it, we have taken a step-by-step approach. You will undoubtedly find that in real life the process will not be as neatly linear and you will be working on many steps at the same time, return to early steps later, and so on.

Part 2 looks first at designing, planning and preparing for teaching groups of learners, before considering these stages in the development of one-to-one ToTing.

Chapter 4

Designing your programme

Introduction

We see a programme for teaching teachers as anything that has a clear beginning and end, and during which ToTs are trying to support the learning of the teacher participants and the achievement of pre-specified purposes. It may therefore range in scale from a four-year, full-time, initial teacher preparation programme for new teachers to a one-day programme to introduce existing teachers to a small-scale local innovation.

Whatever its scope, the programme will need to have a budget. This will need to cover:

- the time of initial needs' analysts and programme designers and planners (who may or may not be the same people as those who will teach on the programme) and time for any post-use revisions and evaluations
- the time for ToTs (in cases where they are not the principal designers) to be involved in these stages of the process, plus the time they need for preparation and their actual teaching, together with time for any prior trainer training needed
- the time of the participants. Will schools need to pay for supply cover?
- travel, accommodation and subsistence for participants and ToTs if needed
- costs of resources – course library, materials development, photocopying, printing, stationery, etc.
- administrative costs – e.g. for obtaining permissions, sending letters to participants, providing support for ToTs

All the above may represent a considerable investment, which makes it all the more important that the programme does the job it was designed to do.

The larger the scale of the design the longer the entire programme development will take and the more likely it is to be part of a wider educational reform process. The primary concern of the designers, especially of those at national level, will frequently be to try to balance the often conflicting demands of the political, economic and social realities and the new ways of thinking introduced by the reform. They may not have much first-hand knowledge about classroom realities, what teachers already know, or what they might want or need to know. However, whatever the scale of the programme each stage below is necessary, requires effort, thought and time to accomplish and will need to be done afresh for each new programme. In addition if you, as a ToT, are asked to work on a programme that has already been designed, and perhaps planned (as is often the case with initial preparation programmes), you need to try to find out as much as possible about the thinking behind that design and planning before going on to your own preparation.

The design of any programme needs to be based on a more or less explicit understanding of three interconnected areas. These are:

- what it is thought teachers need to learn
- what the programme should aim to achieve, and
- what the context requires and is like (both what has prompted the need for the programme, and how such a programme will fit into the existing contextual realities)

Although we discuss needs, aims and contexts separately below, we recognize that decisions made in response to one of these may need to be rethought in the light of influences from the others. This is what makes this process more messy than we can easily demonstrate here.

4.1 Identifying needs

We have seen above that because programmes are often designed by people who are not ToTs, or with little recent first-hand experience of classrooms, programmes do not always reflect an understanding of teachers' actual needs. This is one reason why so many reform efforts fail. The process of identifying needs is fundamental for two reasons. The first is that accurate identification of needs is an essential feature of successful programmes. The second is that programme development is always based on some view of teachers' needs (however accurate or explicitly stated this is) since it affects all decision-making made at all stages. A view of teachers' needs will always be a core part of the answer to the question 'Why have we decided to have this programme?' If a programme is going to have the desired effect (and essentially in most resource-poor educational environments be cost-effective) it must be designed to address genuine needs.

So what do we mean by 'genuine' needs? Learners' needs can be thought of in two overlapping ways. The first and perhaps the most usual way is to think about what it is that the intended participant group lacks. This of course requires detailed specification of who the intended participants will be. This view of what participants lack is most often an outsider perspective in which the programme designer(s) make(s) a judgement about what the target learners do not yet know (in all three senses of the word), but which it is thought essential for them to know if some larger goal (the purpose or initial motivation for the programme) is to be achieved.

Looking at needs purely in terms of 'lacks' is extremely common, particularly if the programme is a national or large-scale one. The idea of lacks is often linked to what targets ('target needs') the programme needs to aim for to be successful, based on the designers' estimated generalization about how far away from the target the teaching population currently is. For example, if a hoped-for outcome of an educational reform includes teachers being more aware of individual differences in their classrooms and it is believed that the majority of teachers are only familiar with teaching in a lockstep fashion, then the 'lacks' will be substantial and the target needs will include knowing about such learner differences, how to discover them and knowing how to manage the classroom in a manner that takes them into account. One frequent outcome of this limited view of needs is that too little time is provided for programmes as a whole, because there are further needs that require consideration at this design stage, and we discuss these next.

A second way of thinking about needs when designing a programme is in terms of conditions required for undertaking the kind of learning that ToTs hope to support. These are sometimes referred to as 'process needs'. For example, if you want participants to learn some new aspect of 'knowing how', they will need time and opportunities for supported trying out. Another example of process needs follows on from this: if learners are to feel comfortable about 'trying out' and making the inevitable mistakes that are part of learning, the programme will need to be designed with the consideration of making them feel generally comfortable both physically and psychologically.

Finally, and related to the process need of making participants feel psychologically comfortable, is the requirement to acknowledge the fact that adult learners in particular need to see the relevance of what they are studying if they are to learn. Therefore teacher learners' subjective needs, sometimes called 'wants', must also be taken into consideration. While 'wants' have important implications for teaching (see below, and 8.1.1, on group dynamics), they may also be directly relevant at the design stage. For example if, as would ideally be the case, ToTs have sought information from potential programme participants and this tells us that what they most want to learn is the use of IT in their subject area, then taking this 'want' into serious consideration will have design and, in particular, resource implications.

For designers to take 'wants' seriously they will need to believe two things. First that it is important to take such 'wants' into consideration because it indicates what the teachers are ready to learn and so will be cost-effective in the long term, and second that skilful planners and implementers will be able to find ways of combining teachers' wants with target needs – e.g. in this case perhaps making the main focus of the programme: Ways of using IT to cater for a variety of learners' differences.

Broadly speaking there can be two different programme design scenarios. In the first ToTs are designing (or participating to some degree in the design of) a course to meet more or less specified targets set by somebody else. In the second scenario they are comparatively free to establish their own targets, bearing the context in mind. For both these scenarios we will suggest questions they might ask themselves and where they might find answers.

Scenario 1 Pre-specified programme targets for pre-specified target learner groups

As a ToT, having established that you know what the targets are and what types of knowledge they involve, the two main questions that follow may help in the needs analysis process that is necessary to determine course content, amount of time needed, how the time will be divided up and what premises will be required. The aim is always to be as fully informed as circumstances allow, so in the table below we suggest ideal and essential versions of the kind of information that might be useful for identifying needs.

Table 1   Possible questions

Possible questions	Ways of finding answers
Which aspects of what the targets require do the participants already know (in all three senses)?	**Ideally**, you would carry out a full baseline survey involving proper sampling of the target population. This would necessarily involve classroom observations and interviews with teachers as well as with pupils, parents, headteachers and local educational professionals who have regular contact with the target population of teachers such as members of the inspectorate. **At the very least**, you will need to introspect (if you are still or were once a teacher in the context) and talk to as many members of the above groups as possible.
Who are the participants? • What programmes have they attended already? • What types of programmes were these? • How did they experience those programmes? • Are they choosing to come to this programme or will they be 'sent'? • What feelings and attitudes will they bring to the programme? • What is the reality of their lives inside and outside teaching? • How much freedom do they have to choose how they spend their time inside and outside the classroom? • What is their socio-economic status as a group and as individuals? And other questions of this kind.	**Ideally**, addressing these questions would involve talking to and shadowing as many members of the target population groups as possible. As well as trying to identify prevailing attitudes and approaches this will involve investigating the economic and professional realities within which such teachers live. You would also investigate documentation about previous programmes, and speak to providers of programmes that members of the target group are likely to have attended. Finally, you would investigate and try to understand how members of the target group of teachers (and the wider society) think about teaching, learning and education. **At the very least**, again you will need to introspect (if you are/have been a teacher yourself), acknowledging the extent to which your experiences are/might have been the same as or different from others, and spend a day with one or more teachers from the target group.

As you will have noticed from the comparative vagueness of our suggestions, these main questions can be answered at many different levels of exactness. Even the most thorough baseline survey carried out over years will have gaps and may be out of date in certain respects when its results are actually used. The important thing is that programme designers think about these questions and consider and use what is known about the answers during the design process. We have found it helpful to make some kind of poster depicting what we know about potential learners on a programme to use as a constant reminder as we make further decisions.

> If you, the reader, are a designer, but are not actually going to do the teaching yourself, it would be a good idea to involve some ToTs who will be teaching in your design team so that they are aware of why the programme is designed as it is, and so that they can inform the design in the light of their experience of teaching on similar programmes.
>
> Designing is often a continuous process, and ToT members of design teams will be invaluable sources of information for post-course revisions of the programme design after they have run a programme once or twice.

Scenario 2 Pre-specified target learner groups but no detailed pre-specified targets

Situations in which we have found ourselves in this kind of scenario include, for example, being put in charge of teacher development within an institution or geographical area and so being expected to design (and plan, prepare and teach) relevant programmes that will, according to the context, either 'help teachers develop', or help them cope with new demands resulting from, for example, a curriculum reform or a negative official evaluation.

Although identifying needs will be similar to the procedures outlined above, anyone designing in such situations will particularly need to understand what the context expects the outcome of 'development' to look like, in order to help identify appropriate target needs for the teachers for whom they are responsible.

Before addressing the two questions above, therefore, in this scenario designers will need to address the following questions. (We assume the designers in scenario 1 would already have considered these, although in reality they are often ignored, or answers are taken for granted).

Table 2 Questions

Question	Ways of finding answers
Which (or which combination) of the five ultimate goals described in Part 1 is the currently accepted norm in the context?	**Ideally these would include:** examining documentation on existing or previous pre-service teacher programmes to see what their aims are asking teachers and ToTs what kinds of knowledge and qualities they think teachers should have looking at how teachers are evaluated and at any documentation from the inspectorate

Question	Ways of finding answers
	that details what a good teacher ought to be like looking at any mid to long-term educational policy planning documents that outline expected future paths for the education system **At the very least**, you would need to think about the question carefully and compare your thoughts with those of one or more other teachers/teachers of teachers.
How appropriate does the currently accepted norm seem to be for the context in which the teachers are or will have to work? Does it seem to need changing in any way? If so how and why? Examples of mismatches between existing and desired/desirable norms: Example 1: The accepted norm is technicist, but the teaching materials expect teachers to make flexible, learner–sensitive decisions. Example 2: The accepted norm does not include any element of the reflective practitioner goal. However, there is evidence of the desirability of introducing such an element if teachers are to develop flexible attitudes to change and become able to manage their own future learning. Example 3: The future goal of educational policy is that learners should become more autonomous, but the current context has a technicist norm for teachers. The technicist goal will have to change as an important aim of the training is likely to be to help learners to become more autonomous themselves.	**Ideally these would include:** informed thinking about what effect the current norm is having on the results of the teaching–learning process in the context reading as widely as possible about alternative viewpoints and possibilities looking at any mid to long-term educational policy planning documents that outline expected future paths for the education system **At the very least**, you would need to think about what effect the norm is having on the results of the teaching–learning process in the context and compare your thoughts with one or more people who are aware of current educational outcomes.

Having answered these questions, designers in such scenarios need to think about what specific knowledge (of each of the three types) is needed in order for teachers to be as acceptable and effective as possible within the context. For example, if developing reflective practitioners is part of the ultimate goal, teachers will need to build up their 'knowing how' in the skill(s) of reflecting. If being a professional is part of the goal then part of what teachers need to learn to be able to do is make their own informed decisions about and for a range of practices. These may include making personal decisions about how to approach the syllabus, choose a textbook or other materials, or making responsive in-class and lesson-planning decisions.

Having developed a greater awareness of what knowledge is needed by teachers to achieve the ultimate goal, designers are then ready to ask and answer the first pair of questions at scenario 1 above.

When answering the above questions for either scenario, designers are likely to end up with a list of lacks and wants and process needs that may be far greater than it is possible to cover in a single programme. In this case, all other things being equal, it makes sense to begin by addressing 'wants' (particularly any that coincide with 'lacks') that programme participants may have expressed. If the time is to be spent on learning (rather that on *covering* a syllabus), process needs (conditions and processes that support the learning of different kinds of knowledge) must be taken into account, since without meeting these no learning that will affect what participants actually go on to do, or do differently, in their classrooms, can occur.

4.2 Identifying programme aims

As mentioned previously the needs analysis process typically results in a long list of items. Most often, therefore, they will need to be prioritized. One way of thinking that has helped us in this process relates to identifying what we call the strength or importance of the need. In order to do this we have found the following task/thinking process useful. It has also been useful in scenario 2 situations when trying to establish the main aim for the programme.

The process is carried out as follows. For each identified 'need', we ask ourselves 'why', and 'why' again and again until we can find no more answers. Those needs for which we find many answers emerge as relatively more important. This is particularly true if the answers we generate appear under each of the following headings: lacks, wants, context, and 'theories'/research findings (for example, on teacher learning, teacher education, teacher knowledge and/or teachers' lives). If we can use all four categories, this suggests that there are many different kinds of reasons for this need, which adds to its importance.

> We'll take an example from a project we both worked on where a need to develop teachers' abilities to make more informed and appropriate decisions in and for the classroom to meet their learners' needs had been identified.
>
> We found several answers to the question 'Why do teachers have this need?' and in the process found a possible focus for our programme. Below we set out some of the answers that we found in terms of lacks, wants, context and theories.

Lacks

An example of an answer that related to *Lacks* was as follows:

Teachers are reluctant to, and do not know how to make informed decisions about their teaching because historically they have always been told what to do. In addition because they have previously been expected to cover every task in the single textbook and finish it by the end of the year, they lack skills and experience in analysing learner needs and using such an analysis to make appropriate choices from among the activities in the textbook.

Wants

An example of an answer relating to *Wants* was that teachers had said in the needs analysis that, although they are now allowed to choose textbooks for themselves, they find it hard to make decisions about which textbook might be the most useful for them. In addition they said that, although they had been told that they should use their textbooks flexibly, according to their learners' needs, they didn't know how to decide which of the activities in the textbooks to use and/or to leave out and/or to adapt. (Observation during the needs analysis showed that teachers in practice used only the textbook as teaching material, and used the units in it exactly as written.)

Context

The new curriculum stipulates that teachers should adapt their teaching to the specific needs of their own learners. Currently this is a very common feature of curriculum reform worldwide. As the extract below indicates it often entails fundamental changes to the skills that teachers need to develop and the range of roles that they are expected to play.

> According to the new curriculum teachers' roles will be very different from the past. Teachers are no longer merely informants of knowledge. In addition to empowering pupils with subject knowledge they are curriculum adaptors. Teachers should decide on the teaching content, design tasks as well as select and develop materials which they think appropriate for their pupils. They are planners scheduling the teaching content and materials (Berry 2003: 4).*

Theories

There are many relevant research findings. For example, these suggest that teachers are happiest and remain in the profession longest when they have a) the freedom, b) the ability and c) the confidence to feel that they can continuously adapt what they do in the classroom to the needs of their learners. (This may have influenced the original policy decision to encourage teachers to be more autonomous, as there are retention issues within the profession in this context.)

If a need is really important, then there will be answers in each of the four areas (usually several answers). This helps us determine that this need must be addressed in the proposed programme.

Once the decision to address this need on the programme has been made, a further round of questioning, in which the above answers become a new set of 'why' questions' may be helpful in deciding how to design the programme.

* See References, p.98.

For example, we saw under '*Wants*' above that teachers find it difficult to make decisions between textbooks, so we asked ourselves why this was so ('Why do teachers find it difficult to make decisions between textbooks?').

Useful answers for the design process included:

- Because initial teacher preparation has not included work on textbook analysis and evaluation (so we could not assume any prior KA in this. If the needs analysis data confirm this, it has design implications. We would need to take this into consideration when establishing realistic targets for the time available).
- Because the educational culture is one in which traditionally knowledge has been transmitted from 'experts', and teachers were recipients rather than generators of such knowledge (so we would need consider what might be needed to support such attitudinal change in our design – e.g. one-to-one ToTing (see Chapter 7), and as much time as possible).

And we can again go behind each of these, for example: 'Why has initial teacher preparation not included work on textbook analysis and evaluation?'

Among the answers at this depth of questioning came the thought that, for some of the contextual and historical reasons outlined above, local ToTs did not know how to do it themselves and so could not help others to learn how to do it. This then could explain why we, as non-local ToTs had been asked to work on the programme, and had further design implications when considering staffing and the participants on the first course. Should local ToTs be involved in the programme? In what ways? Should all or the majority of participants be teachers or local ToTS?

So where does all this leave us?

If we have answers to 'WHY' questions in each of the four categories and additionally a number of answers 'behind' each initial reason (as illustrated above) then *this* need is indeed 'high priority'. Also because (as is frequently the case when participants are expected to implement a new educational reform) this need includes an attitudinal change (from reluctance to willingness to be flexible) and skills development, it will take a long time to address. For all of these reasons it will be important to try to begin to meet this need in the programme we are designing.

This process of identification of important needs may, as we have seen, help ToTs to make many important design decisions, as long as they are in a position to do so. These include:

- how long the programme will be
- the format of the programme – is it one 3-week session or three 1-week sessions over a longer period with time back in schools in between?
- the sorts of premises that will be needed
- the sorts of ToTs that will be needed

- the composition of participant groups

To illustrate this

- if the needs require a ToT with specific skills, such as textbook evaluation or test design, then these must be identified and 'booked' either locally or from the wider national or international professional community
- if learners need to develop reflective skills, then the format of the course is likely to require a format that allows regular periods of time in school interspersed by periods of group time (see Part 1 for conditions for learning different kinds of knowledge)

Clearly, if the above design decisions are made by designers who have had no part in identifying important needs, then when ToTs come to plan and prepare they are likely to find themselves (as in fact is often the case) in a working environment that is less than ideal. This will have (usually unhelpful) implications for the ultimate outcome of the programme as a whole.

4.3 The influence of context on design decisions

Before we go on to talk about planning, we want to say a little more about context. Aspects of context have already appeared in the needs analysis process. However, thinking about the 'elephant' of designing from the aspect of context may sometimes be a helpful check on the 'fit' of the proposed programme for the place, time and the people that it is supposed to benefit. Examples of contextual realities that may affect the design stage include:

- A minimum number of days/hours officially required for an in-service programme to 'count' for a teacher's required professional development quota and/or promotion.
- Particular cultural sensitivities resulting from religious or political factors that may influence the training formats or group compositions that are possible.
- Particular educational ideas and language that are current either within a national system or the educational world more generally. Currently fashionable terms, in our fields at least, include for example 'problem-based learning' , 'task-based learning', 'multiple intelligences', 'learner-centredness', 'assessment for learning' 'personalization', 'behaviour management', 'blended learning' and so on.
- The rhythms of the school year and the acceptability (or not) of planning programmes for school holidays.
- The availability of ToTs with the requisite skills within the environment and whether it is possible – politically or financially – to look more widely if need be.
- The prevailing educational approach – how the majority of teachers think

about the purpose of education, about their subject, about how it is learnt and how it is appropriate to teach it. (The further away this is from the desired outcomes of the programme, the longer the programme will need to be and the less likely it is that aims will be achieved in a single stage.)

If you have imagined yourself going through all the above stages in an 'ideal' way, you will see that this will be a very time-consuming process. It is important to remember that the purpose of this finding out is to expose yourself to the kinds of experience and information that will help you to make appropriate decisions for your context. There is a sense in which all our decisions are 'spur of the moment', rather than the result of pure rational analysis, and the process outlined above, carried out as fully as possible given the circumstances you are in, will provide information and experiences which will guide your own final 'gut' design decisions (see 'modes of mind' in Chapter 3). Going through this process is then ultimately a matter of preparing yourself for the practice of designing. We now move on the next stage in the programme development process.

Chapter 5

Planning

In this chapter we begin by discussing the planning stage in developing programmes for work with groups of teachers.

At this stage of the process planners (who have hopefully also been designers) have to make decisions with regard to which need is going to be addressed when in the programme, how this might be done and how much time would be needed. The starting point will be the outcome of the decisions made at the design stage. To illustrate the starting point of an imaginary planning process we will again take the context discussed in Chapter 4 where it was identified that teachers needed support in meeting the requirement that they should make more independent decisions in the light of their learners' needs.

At the design phase, it was decided that there was only funding for a 6-day programme, given that the participants would come from all over the country, and that it would therefore need to be residential. It was further decided that the programme would consist of two residential 3-day blocks interspersed by time in schools for participants to try things out in their real contexts. The two 3-day blocks would be based at a Teachers' Centre in the capital. Between each block teachers would spend four weeks back in their own classrooms. Given the time available decisions had to be made about *which* decision-making processes to focus on. Here the background *why* information helped in deciding that the focus would be on using the textbook. The reasoning for this went as follows: teachers had said they find it hard to make decisions between textbooks which they are now allowed to choose *and* when we looked further and asked why teachers find it difficult to make decisions between textbooks we found, for example, that they had never been expected or allowed to do so in the past and therefore hadn't developed the skills of doing so. In addition for most teachers decisions about textbooks are still made at school or district/county/region level. All teachers nonetheless *use* textbooks and were being encouraged to do so more flexibly. Therefore, textbook evaluation and analysis might initially best be introduced by helping teachers make informed decisions about how to use the textbook they already have rather than by choosing between different textbooks. Given all that was known about teachers' wants, lacks and the reasons behind them (in terms of curriculum expectations, etc.), it was decided that the focus of the programme would be *Using your textbook more effectively to support your learners' learning.*

You will notice that in the above example 'process' needs have not been mentioned. In order to begin to take them into consideration we have found, at this planning stage too, that it is helpful to ask ourselves further questions, answers to which help make the plan much clearer. Whereas at the design stage (Chapter 4) we looked *behind* the identified need when we asked and answered our 'why-questions', in planning to consider process needs we move *forward* from the identified lacks and wants-derived need (in this case 'for teachers to learn how to meet the requirement that they should make more independent decisions in the light of their pupils' learning needs') to imagine and consider a number of 'how-questions'. The purpose of this is to work out how ToTs might address the need and when and where this might best be done on the programme.

As an example, using the same context we ask the following: 'How can ToTs help teachers develop the abilities to make independent, appropriate decisions in their classrooms to meet their pupils' learning needs?'

Here again a number of answers can be generated such as:

Answer 1: by helping them realize which decisions they already make whether consciously or not and when and why they make them (for example, in choosing what language to use when giving instructions, giving additional explanations, commenting on learner behaviour, etc.).

Answer 2: by identifying what information of what kind they currently use in making decisions and why.

Answer 3: by helping them understand the kinds of information (and content of that information), that others use in decision-making.

Answer 4: by ensuring that they know about and use strategies for assessing learning, learners and their own teaching.

Answer 5: by ToTs scaffolding (see Chapter 9) learner-teachers' actual decision-making processes for their classroom.

These have the following implications for planning:

Answers 1 and 2 remind us that time will need to be allowed early in the programme for ToTs to help participants to discover what decisions they already make, as well as why, how and when they make them.

Answer 3 suggests that input on what informs decision-making (with respect to textbook use) will be needed on the programme.

Answers 4 and 5 suggest that a considerable amount of time will need to be blocked to support participants in skill development and the pro-gramme design will ideally incorporate at least one phase back in the real classroom.

As you can see in the example above, further 'design' implications may emerge at this stage. Here, for example, answers 4 and 5, in particular, suggest the need for a design format that includes participants spending some time in their own classrooms, perhaps with one-to-one ToT support. If the designers of the programme have not taken this into consideration, it may or may not be possible to revise the design at this stage. If it is not, the real classroom experiences that would be most desirable will have to be simulated, imagined, recalled and so on in a variety of 5-step processes, and perhaps some kind of peer-support network set up for post-programme use. This again highlights the desirability of designers and planners being the same people.

The answering of the above planning questions enables a rough 'blocking' of topics and processes within the time available, as well as a clearer specification of the aims and focus of the programme. In doing this rough blocking we have found it useful to think of vertical strands and horizontal threads, the former relating to KA and the latter to KH and KT development work. In other words the programme documentation may seem to be organized in terms of KA-like topics, but within these the plan needs to take account of the time needed for completing '5-step' processes (see Chapter 3) as well as the development of skills. As discussed in Chapter 2 skill learning requires repeated opportunities for participants to try out, and so become aware of what they do and do not know or know how to do. This inevitably affects planning, and in particular highlights the need to plan 'unplanned' slots to respond to the potentially less predictable outcomes of such trying-out processes. We try to show what we mean by this in the example below:

As a stage in a skill-learning process relating to textbook adaptation, you have asked participants to adapt a particular part of a textbook to make it more suitable for a particular group of young learners from a certain background with a defined existing level of knowledge. The participants decide, appropriately it would seem, that it would be good to adapt a piece of text into a story format that they can then tell. It becomes clear when they try this for the first time that they lack information about narrative structure and the differences between written and spoken language. The ToT uses what they have noticed to decide what these participants are ready to learn next. The ToT then provides input on narrative structure, and on the differences between spoken and written language as well as further opportunities for storytelling practice.

As the example shows, planning needs to be fairly flexible both in terms of content and of timing, since it is impossible to be certain in advance precisely what information will emerge from these practice stages. One useful 'trick' we have developed for planning for this is to schedule the initial trying-out sessions for the end of a day, so that we have time before the next session to make decisions about how to respond and to prepare accordingly.

In addition further process needs will require attention at this planning stage, with time allocated at the start of the course, for example, for goal setting, getting to know each other and group-forming activities, as well as at the end for group disbanding (see Chapter 8, group dynamics).

When we plan we also draw on principles (some of which we have already referred to) derived from our understandings of what teachers need to know, how they learn these things and how we can support them in their learning. We bear the following in mind:

1. 'get out before you put in'
2. 'begin and end with experience'
3. KH and KT development takes time
4. we may need to allow time for teachers to become aware that they need to know what we want them to KA
5. process needs (e.g. creating a psychologically safe environment) are important and will take time to address
6. in a multi-site format (e.g. the Teachers' Centre and the classroom) ToTs need to be clear about which parts of which learning sequences occur at each site and how they relate to each other
7. addressing some needs (or aspects of these) may only be possible after others have been dealt with

We try to reflect these principles in the following example rough plan for the imaginary programme we have been using throughout this Part. The plan is not exactly as we would actually draft it. For example, we would not include the information in brackets, where the numbers refer back to the principles above.

Table 3 Block one

	Day 1 Starting points	Day 2 Making textbooks locally relevant	Day 3 Preparing to try it in your classroom
Session 1	Group formation [process needs P2 & 5, 7]	Sharing and comparing responses to evening task. Implications [P1 'getting out' and getting reactions from others – P4]	Sharing as Day 2 [P1 and P4]
Session 2	How you use your textbooks now [P1 & 2 getting out focus on past experience]	3 questions to consider, when making decisions about using the textbook [P1 planned input]	How do you know if you have made the right decisions? [P1 getting out and putting in]
Lunch			

	Day 1 Starting points	Day 2 Making textbooks locally relevant	Day 3 Preparing to try it in your classroom
Session 3	One view of possible options: adopt, adapt, supplement [P1 – planned input]	Task: textbook extract: What would you do with this and why? [P3 trying out] (access to a range of supplementary material – P3,4 & 7, now that they can see that they might need these)	Preparation for trying again in the real classroom. P2 and 3 Getting evidence to evaluate decisions (focus on future experience) Group dinner (P5)
Evening	Poster of your 'typical learner' – what they know/can do + what they don't + what they like/don't etc.		

(Four weeks spent back in the classroom with structured reflective action tasks involving the trying out of new ways of using text book materials with their own learners, and gathering evidence of possible impact of such new ways of working.)

	Day 4 So what happened?	Day 5 Making it work in real life	Day 6 Where next?
Session 1	Group reforming [process needs]	'Yes buts'–contextual opportunities and constraints deriving from experience of classroom practice. Difficulties in real classrooms/schools. [getting out and shared inputs]	As decided Day 5
Session 2	Analysing evidence gathered by learners during the classroom block to assess effectiveness of decisions [getting out – focus on past experience]	Development of new shared goals based on the above and evening work [process needs] *either* more trying out [with new textbook extracts in small groups] *or* more on what counts as evidence of effectiveness of planning decisions *or* analysis/	Role play: teacher who uses textbook as it is teacher who makes decisions about textbook content [imagining future experience]

	Day 4 So what happened?	Day 5 Making it work in real life	Day 6 Where next?
		interpretation of evidence gathered in classrooms *or* strategies for dealing with 'Yes buts' [trying out and/or putting in]	
Lunch			
Session 3	As Session 2	As decided above	Group disbanding and final party Group dinner [process needs]
Evening	Using outcomes of Sessions 2 and 3 for individual assessment of effectiveness of decisions made and what has been learned from them [identifying remaining wants and needs]		

We said earlier that the written outline is more likely to emphasize the vertical strands (KA) either in terms of the topic of the day or the title of sessions. For example, on Day 1, session 3 in the field of language teaching there are people who write about 'the need to and how to adopt, adapt and supplement textbooks and reasons why these decisions might be made'. In our minds in this imaginary plan this is where the ToT would talk about other people's views as well as asking participants to go back to their discussion in session 2 and consider whether any of the 'input' might be relevant to them.

However, unlike more traditional plans, not all of our headings are 'vertical'. Others such as 'Starting points (Day 1), 'Where next?' (Day 6) relate to group processes, while yet others like the reflective action tasks back in the classroom or the Day 2 session 3 task, relate to developing the skills of textbook analysis and adaptation to meet local needs. In relation to skill development you will also notice that on the plan for the second block the content of the various sessions is vaguer and there are more 'or' possibilities (Day, 5 session 2) since this depends more on the skill-learning process and the stage that the participants have reached, and also the contextual issues that have arisen as they have tried things out back in the classroom. This illustrates the notion of planning 'unplanned' sessions.

This is a plan that we would feel comfortable working with. However, if this is your first time as a ToT, your gut instinct may be to try and define exactly what you are going to do from Day 1 to Day 6 more precisely. When we have felt like this, and we still do on occasions, we try to remember to 'trust the process', and to act on our intellectual belief that we can trust ourselves and our participants. For example, second blocks of programmes such as the one above need 'unplanned planning', because participants will all be returning with different experiences which they will not only need and want to share, which is 'plannable', but also with new needs and wants which are much less predictable. So we do try not to over-plan, because when we do, we make the corresponding preparations (see below) and so tend to be reluctant not to use what we have spent so much time preparing, even when we shouldn't because it is not really needed or wanted, and something else entirely might be more appropriate. On courses such as the one above where the focus is on enabling participants to become more responsive to their pupils' learning needs, it is particularly important that ToTs model such a responsive approach with their learners (remembering that the whole programme is a UFO! See Chapter 3). One of the conditions for this to be possible is that the plan has appropriate 'unplanned' blocks.

We said above that ToTs need to trust themselves if they are going to work with such a flexible and open plan. To do this, they need to feel secure and confident. Having taken part in the designing and planning of the programme, and so understanding the thinking behind it, will boost confidence. In addition, it is helpful if ToTs do not find themselves in the position of having to teach any skills that they have not got themselves, or talk about conceptual tools that they have not personally found practically useful in thinking about their teaching. Another way to feel more secure about the 'vague' parts of the plan, especially in its later stages, is to find materials and information to have in 'store' for use if and when it proves helpful to do so.

Another issue we have encountered with 'vague' plans is that participants and sponsors do expect to be given a clear and possibly full written plan. This is not difficult to construct, but we strongly suggest that this is given with a proviso that the actual content and sequence might change (according to the needs emerging from the group process and skill-learning threads).

Chapter 6

Preparation

Once you have got your plan, there are still other things that need to be done before you can actually teach. We see preparation as being of two kinds: concrete preparation and preparation of self and, although for linear convenience we are talking about this phase here, in fact all of the work you have done so far will have contributed to it and some of the things we are going to suggest here may well have started much earlier in the process.

6.1 Concrete preparation

We start with the concrete preparation by which we mean (in a likely time sequence) things such as:

1. identifying and booking ToTs and facilities
2. identifying and notifying participants
3. obtaining necessary permissions and ensuring that any other administrative or logistic requirements are met
4. gathering materials
5. writing detailed session plans
6. creating handouts, reading packs and resources
7. organizing any necessary photocopying or printing
   as well as last-minute preparations such as:
8. arranging the room
9. and ensuring that as far as possible all necessary day-to-day facilities are in place and functioning

Of the above list items 1–3 and 7 are so context-specific that we are unable to discuss them further. We include them in the list above because we have found it important to check whether designers and planners have already done them (when we have not been involved at these stages ourselves) or to remember to do them ourselves or make sure somebody else does. We now look at numbers 4–6 and 8–9 one by one.

6.1.1 Gathering materials

By the term 'materials' here we mean both books and articles relating to the vertical strand (KA) topics that are planned or might be needed, as well as, on pre-existing courses, any of the readings or handouts that previous ToTs have used. There are two purposes in gathering materials. One is to inform yourself and prepare to respond to emerging needs, especially during the vaguer end of course phase (as we saw above), and the other is to use them or ideas from them in the preparation of handouts and for the session-design process.

Where can you find them? If you have Internet access there is an enormous amount of information available, but we have learnt to be cautious about relying only on these sources since it is hard to be sure how reliable what you find there is. There are, of course, some sites which are more carefully controlled and trust-worthy, and one way of being more sure about how reliable Internet information is, is to follow the advice given about useful websites in your subject-specific journals. Also it is worth remembering that the vast majority of the online information in English is written by people working in education systems in the USA, the UK, Canada or Australia and so the experiences on which they are based may be very different from those typically found in your context. While they may well provide a very useful perspective, you will need to take this contextual issue into consideration.

Designers of new courses will hopefully have included provision for resources in the budget, which may allow you to buy a course library, and major publishers such as Continuum, Routledge-Falmer, Oxford and Cambridge University Presses, or whichever international or national publisher is best known for your subject, can be contacted through the net to obtain appropriate catalogues. Since your budget (if you have one) will almost certainly be limited, you will need to keep both the programme purpose and plan clearly in mind as you select which books to order. In addition, on many courses some materials are primarily for the trainer, while others are intended to be distributed to participants. This also needs to be considered when gathering materials.

If you are in a context where the course has run before and there are copies of handouts that others have written and used it is tempting to think that they can be reused with little or no adjustment. However, they were always written by someone else with different participants in mind and perhaps for slightly different purposes. It may be hard (depending on the type of handout – see below) to understand what exactly the purpose was, and you may or may not have infor-mation about how well it was felt that the purpose was achieved. These handouts may, though, be very useful resources for ideas about task types, and examples that you can adapt for your own purposes. We like to read them through and try and imagine the plan of the course as it actually happened with that group, and at the same time identify parts of the existing handouts that we feel will be relevant to our plan and might therefore be reused by us. (In a sense this is an example of 'textbook analysis and adaptation'.)

6.1.2 Preparing detailed session plans

Just as the main purpose of sessions on lesson planning in initial teacher preparation is to teach us a way of thinking, rather than to provide a detailed model for us to follow exactly for the rest of our professional careers, the same is true with session-plan formats. However, the example we are proposing here is a format that, although it was particularly useful when we began teaching teachers, we still use on occasions.

We start out by getting one A4 sheet of paper marked up as below:

Course Day Session Aims:					
Timing	Activity name and type	Org.	Basic needs	Materials	Mats check

The information at the top is fairly self-explanatory and provides a record of what was done on what course on what day and in which session. However, we'd like to say a word or two more about aims. By aims, we mean what you as ToTs are aiming to achieve in any given session. Having the aims in front of you is a constant reminder of what you are planning the session for. In addition, thinking through clear and specified aims is an important part of 'preparation of self' (see below). ToT aims, of course, are based on considerations of desired 'target needs', such as, in this case, helping teachers develop greater flexibility in how they use their textbooks. We prefer to stipulate 'ToT aims' rather than the 'learning objectives' specified as necessary to meet 'target needs' to remind ourselves (during session planning and preparation of self in particular) of the part we as individual ToTs play in helping participants learn, through the decisions we make both at this session-planning phase and during our teaching. We also have several further reasons for talking, on our session plans, in terms of 'ToT aims' rather than 'learning objectives'.

Most ToTs will want to start each session by outlining what is in the session and what its purpose is, and using our aims can help us do that. If this is expressed in terms of learning objectives this may have a number of negative consequences. First the participants may be so focused on the specified objectives that they are not open to learning other unpredictable things that may be provided by, for example, fellow participants. Secondly, they may feel bad or inadequate, if by the end of the session they feel they have not in fact achieved the objectives (regardless of whether it was realistic to expect them to do so). Finally pre-specified learning objectives are often used to evaluate sessions and typically participants, if asked what they have learned, will want to please the ToT and so parrot back the words of the learning objectives, so – as with leading questions in interviews or questionnaires – giving an unreliable indication of what has actually been achieved.

Back to our session-planning template above. In the Timing column we enter the estimated end time of each task, phase or activity. This is because we use the finished session plan as a guide during the session (an important reason for keeping it to one side of A4) and have found that this helps us keep track of timing. The Activity column is where we put a title or name for the task, activity or phase of the session and its 'type' in terms of the five steps discussed in Chapter 3 ((1) describing experience – (2) explaining – (3) having access to other explanations – (4) reconsidering – (5) planning for future experience). We put a star next to any activities which could be adapted or left out if earlier stages take longer than we anticipate and, although we rarely need it in our experience, we also add at least one activity to the bottom of the column in case things take less time than we expect. Under 'Org.' we indicate the type of classroom organization needed for the phase which might be WG (whole group – one person is talking – usually the ToT – everyone else listening), SG (small group), I (individual), PW (pair work), M (mingle). This helps us check that we have variety and, when we have SG or PW written in the column, reminds us to think about whether we need a random pairing/grouping activity beforehand or will assign pairs/groups. The next column, Basic needs, refers to the basic psychological needs referred to in Chapter 2 (F – fun, SUC – success, B – belonging, C – choices, SEC – security), again to check that there are opportunities for all of these to be met, if not all in one session then at least across a number of sessions. In the Materials column we list the materials needed for each phase, task or activity, and the final Check column we use at the last minute when preparing to go in to teach to tick off that we have in fact got all those materials with us.

Below we give two examples, a first draft and a final draft of what the session plan might look like for the first session of our imaginary programme above. We assume we have 30 participants, and a flat room with movable chairs/tables. For the purposes of demonstration we have exaggerated the differences between the two versions.

Table 4 Initial Draft

Course: *Using your textbook more effectively to support your learners' learning.*					
Day 1					
Session 1 8.30–10.30					
Aims: • to start the group process • to provide examples of various ways of thinking about the relationship between textbooks, teachers and learners					
Timing	Activity name and type	Org.	Basic needs	Materials	Mats check
8.50	Welcome. ToT intro including explanation of goals of programme	WG	SEC	Programme	
9.00	Taking the register	WG		List of participants	
10.00	Self presentations	WG		none	
10.30	Some views on the roles of materials from the literature	WG		Handout and references	

Looking at this initial draft we see we have some problems. This is first apparent because we do not know how to fill in the basic needs column and also the whole two hours is organized in the same WG manner. We are pleased because we think we have got the timing right, but do worry that there is not enough variety and also about whether we would really have started to develop any sense of 'group' if we organize things in this way.

We go back to the literature that discusses group dynamics (see Chapter 8) and phases of group life and read that there are three important things to do in any group-forming stage.

- To allow people to get to know each other.
  We think we've done that through the self presentations, but worry that people might feel a bit awkward standing up in front of a room full of strangers, and so the basic need of security would not be met.
- To form group norms, that is ways of working together, and making clear what we can expect from each other (including the tutor).
  We see that we have given ourselves (the ToTs) some time, when explaining the programme, to make some of our own expectations clear, but there is no time for the participants to do so.
- To develop shared goals.
  We look at the plan again and see that, although we have talked about goals, they have been our goals and we've done nothing to establish *shared* goals.

Also, we remember the needs-analysis process and realize we have forgotten to plan a way of getting some idea of the subjective needs or wants of this *particular* group of participants. We make a note that next time, as soon as we know who the participants are, we will write to them as early as possible, and ask them, hopefully before we finalize the programme plan. (An example of the kind of thing we use, adapted for this imaginary programme, is given in Chapter 7, p. 94.)

We decide to reword our first aim to remind us of the things that need to be done and, given there had been a problem with the first, to look again at our second aim. Here we see that the way we've phrased our second aim has led us to plan to give examples of how 'experts' in the literature view the relationships. In planning to do so at this stage, we have forgotten the 'get out before you put in' principle and have not planned to spend any time finding out what the participants views are first. We need to rethink this and perhaps postpone our input until Session 2, after they have had a chance to say what they think, and we have had a chance to understand what ideas and preconceptions they are bringing with them.

Table 5   Final Version

Course: *Using your textbook more effectively to support your learners' learning.*

Day 1

Session 1 8.30–10.30

Aims:

- To start the group process focus on
  - inter-member relationships
  - group norms
  - shared goals:
  - to explore group beliefs about the relationship between textbooks, teachers and learners

Timing	Activity name and type	Org.	Basic needs	Materials	Mats check
8.45	Welcome. ToT intro	WG	SEC	Programme	
9.05	Name game (1)	Circle	F + B+ SEC	Soft ball	
9.35	Get a new chair (1, 2, 3)	Circle Mingle	F + B		
9.45	Experience line-up	Mingle			
10.15	Goal setting 2	I to SG to WG	B + SEC		
10.30	The materials used this morning 2*	SG	SUC	Task handout	

You will see that we have starred this final task. As explained above, this means we think it's possible (even likely!) we will not able to complete this during this session. Thinking this through is something that occurs in 'preparation of self', which we will discuss in the following section.

Before you read on you might want to look at the fuller description of the activities we have chosen that are given at the end of this section, in order to help you imagine what might actually happen in the session, which is what a ToT actually needs to do when they are planning.

You will see that this final version is entirely different. It has, for example, a variety of classroom-organization formats which, apart from providing variety, also will allow work on 'inter-member relationships' as participants will find themselves working with a number of others, observing others at play and forming impressions and so on. You will also see that there is variety in the Basic-needs column. How did we achieve this? First we wanted to find a less threatening and more fun way of learning each other's names, and remembered a game from our language-teaching background (see fuller description below) which involved everyone, including the ToT standing in a circle and throwing a ball around. This would also provide opportunities for laughter and fun and thus begin to 'break the ice'. It would provide an experience of a kind of activity that could be used in classrooms. The fact that the ToT joins in the game could send a 'message of 'equality', and shows that the ToT too is fundamentally a teacher (and learner) rather than a detached theoretical expert. Despite what beginner ToTs might think, it is this evidence of teacherly ability that for many teachers lends a ToT authority. The next activity (in which the ToT also participates) was selected in order to provide opportunities for further fun and ice-breaking as well as reinforcement of the role and valid 'authority' of the ToT.

However, the main purpose for selecting this activity was to provide an experience (as the first step in a five-step sequence) on the basis of which discussions about some group norms and expectations could be held, as well as to raise awareness of the need for specified individual and group goals which would be explored in the subsequent tasks. Yet, as these subsequent tasks would eventually require participants to work in small groups, we decided to include a random-grouping activity next. The choice of precise activity was made to emphasize expected norms and roles, as it would result in a whole-group total number of years of experience of teaching within the room (often something very impressive in the hundreds). This allows the ToT to make the point that it would be pretty silly to ignore that and depend only on their own, comparatively paltry number of years of experience; and so it is expected that all participants will contribute.

In the following goal-setting tasks, participants would be asked to sit in groups (counted off from the previous line-up) and a pyramid discussion (from individual work through small group to reporting back to the whole group) would result in a set of group-generated goals for their learning on the programme. These, seen as 'subjective needs', would then be useful in guiding preparation for future sessions, and important in helping participants gain a sense of success from the programme overall, through their use in the final disbanding phase to 'review learning' as well as through the links the ToT may be able to make to them throughout the programme. The final task, designed to begin to address the second aim, builds on the experience of the morning to explore what we might mean by 'materials', which, if any, are essential to promote learning and so on. (And the ToT would be able to make the point that there were no 'textbook materials' used in the session, but they nonetheless hoped that some 'learning' will have occurred.) The task handout might look something like this:

In your groups, discuss and agree:

A

What you have learnt this morning

What was essential in helping you learn these things

What 'materials' were used to help you learn these things

How they helped your learning

B

Agree on a diagram or visual representation of the relationship between learners, teachers, materials and learning.

You may remember we said in the General Introduction that we hope you will read this book – as we are trying to write it – as a kind of 'dialogue at a distance'. If this is so, you will by now doubtless have 'responded' many times (at least in thought) to what you are reading. Some of these thoughts may have taken the form of 'Well, that's all very well in theory, but . . . ', or 'Yes, but . . . ' (Similarly learners on TL programmes will have such thoughts – and it is useful to help them articulate these.) We are prompted to add this aside now, because we feel some of you, looking at our drafts may be thinking quite big 'Yes, buts . . . ' We have tried to anticipate some of these below.

Yes, but . . .

Looking at the two drafts above you might think that, in reality, it is highly unlikely that the same ToT would produce both of them, and we would agree with you. The first reflects, we think, quite a typical example of the kinds of practices found in programmes for teachers worldwide. It is consistent with a broadly transmission-based, theory–application approach to the teaching–learning process, and might represent a taken for granted, experientially learnt view of appropriate relationships between ToT and participant, which mirrors the roles expected of teachers and learners in the classrooms. Also, ToTs drafting such a plan would be unlikely to have independently selected or created the session-plan template used. This makes the first draft look even more artificial. As with new teachers, new ToTs are likely to adhere to existing norms more firmly than more experienced colleagues since they are keen to demonstrate that they can be/are authoritative ToTs (even if they don't really feel that they are). Some readers will find their first attempts at devising session plans, whatever template they use, are more like the first example above than the second. This is unsurprising, even normal. If people don't have any support in becoming a ToT, what else can they rely on but their previous experience of being a teacher and on occasions a participant on teachers' programmes? If this experience, as is the case in many places, has been in a transmission mode within a theory–application approach, then inevitably your first attempts will reflect this. What we hope we have demonstrated here, through writing about the thinking leading from one draft to the next, is how to *use* the ideas in Part 1 (which, remember, we called '*tools*') to devise plans that are more likely to help teachers to learn in ways that will really change their teaching. The various columns on the template have evolved over time, and we added them to remind *ourselves* to use these ideas, because just like anyone else we find it hard to remember all the things that there are to think about. We, as more 'veteran' ToTs, do have the advantage of having a kitbag of ideas and resources for tasks and activities gathered over many years (at the end of this Part we will describe a few of these as well as how and where you might find others). However, even if your kitbag is not yet as full as ours, you can still plan a session in principle. Then, because you have clear aims for the session and understand what step is missing, can see which needs should still be catered for and what form of classroom organization might best balance the session, you have a lot of information to guide you when searching for a suitable task/activity to fill the holes.

Other readers might look at the second plan and wonder how it could possibly work with their groups that normally number over a hundred. The answer is, of course, it couldn't! At least not as it is, but bearing the aims as well as all the principles and tools in mind, it is possible to devise a plan that might work. One way of achieving similar aims with groups of about 100, for example, is to select (perhaps on the basis of your initial subjective needs analysis letter – see below) four group leaders whose main role is to help with the classroom management. So, for example, for the final draft of the session above, assuming that there is a flat space that is large enough, four groups could be working in parallel. The final aim (and associated task) would then definitely need to move to the second session because, with a group of this size, everything will take quite a lot longer and in particular with complex activities that group leaders themselves might not understand (the Get a new chair game) it will be necessary to demonstrate first with one group of, say, 25 before the others do it, or – less good because there is no substitute for actual personal experience in teacher learning – have one group carry out the activity and the others be observers. Here the process of getting 75 people into position for observing also takes time and thought. We say this not just in theory, but from personal experience of running a very similar session (and 2-week programme) with a group of 120, using group leaders as above.

What if you not only have 100 or more participants but you have also been given a room with fixed chairs and tables in immovable rows? Here again it is a matter of remembering what your aims are and thinking about what it *is* possible to do to try and meet them as fully as possible. So, for example, you might meet the inter-member relationship aim by getting participants to use break times with pre-assigned tasks to get people to know each other better (perhaps you might set the task: 'Find out the name and how long it took to travel to the programme for everyone in your row by the end of the break', and ask participants to sit in the order of 'distance travelled' on their return from the break). In effect here what you are trying to do is to begin to form a group of each row as a start to the wider whole-group forming process. In this case you might want also to make use of whole-group symbols (such as the development of a distinctive name for the particular group – see, e.g., Hadfield 1992*) to develop a feeling of membership. You will probably want to make greater use of pair work in such a setting, and as long as you take care to devise tasks that will result in 'rows' being mixed up in different ways, participants will at least have the opportunity to get to know a range of their colleagues within the smaller row group during the process of the programme.

We cannot predict all the circumstances in which you will find yourselves, but in all the varied environments in which we have found ourselves, what we have hung on to is the idea of trying to achieve our aims using the conceptual *tools* that we have presented here. While our initial reaction to some of the settings may have been dismay, they have provided opportunities for us to develop new and unconventional strategies for achieving what we have increasingly realized are actually often very similar aims.

Some of you may react to the final draft above with the thought, that 'Yes, but ours is also an academic programme leading to a formal degree qualification'. For all the reasons set out in Part 1, we feel that, even within such a programme, if teacher preparation/development is a significant aim, an approach that takes account of current understanding of teacher learning is essential. In such instances, if you are in a sufficiently senior position to make things happen, it may be useful to plan the programme in terms of strands in which those teaching the more formally academic topics can continue to do so as normal, while those responsible for the more directly teacher preparation oriented aspects of the degree have the chance to think carefully about how they might integrate ideas about teacher learning into their approach. In this scenario what is 'put in' after the 'getting out', for example, might involve the ToT in asking the participants to consider (or themselves highlighting) how the KA inputs from the more academic strands may connect with, help to explain or provide a useful conceptual tool in relation to the teaching–learning or other types of experiences being investigated.

Having tried to anticipate some of the 'Yes, but' feelings you might have had looking at the draft session plans above, we now go back to the business of preparing detailed session plans.

For us, one of the trickiest aspects of session planning, perhaps because in a

---

* See References, p. 98.

theory application approach we did not have to think about it, is to decide what the starting point experience might be. This is also partly because ToTs have a range of options to choose from. How then can an appropriate choice be made? We find it helpful to bear three main things in mind: the nature of the input that we hope to be able to make at Step 3; the type of knowledge, KA, KH or KT, which is the main focus of the sequence; the types of experiences already used as starting points on the course so far. We'll say a bit more about each of these next.

The nature of the input that ToTs hope to be able to make at Step 3

ToTs need to be sure that the chosen experience is likely to provide descriptions and explanations that will be about the same kind of thing (an elephant not a tiger) that they hope to be able to deal with in the learning sequence. In considering this we find Shulman's list (see Chapter 1) of the different types of knowledge a teacher needs helpful. For example, ToTs may want to provide some input on techniques for teaching the subject your learners teach (Schulman's content pedagogic knowledge) and may at first think that asking learners to recall a teaching experience would be a suitable starting point. However, in our experience, the stories teachers, particularly in-service learners, tell about their teaching are much more likely to give rise to discussions of a 'general pedagogic knowledge' nature (such as issues of classroom management, the effects of exams, relationships between learners or teachers and learners and so on). These experiences would not then be a suitable starting point for your purposes, and an in-class demonstration (see below) might be more appropriate.

The type of knowledge, KA, KH or KT, which is the main focus of the sequence (see chart below)

The type of knowledge the ToTs want to work on will affect what aspects of the experience you want your learners to describe. However well the ToTs have chosen the type of experience, what learners actually describe will depend on what they notice (which in turn – see Parts 3 and 4 – depends on a number of other factors). Therefore, at the beginning especially, ToTs may also have to help the learners notice certain salient features of the experience which are relevant to the planned learning sequence. It is crucial here to remember that 'help' does not mean 'tell them' what to notice (or what you have noticed). As a quick example here, rather than saying 'Did you notice X ?' a ToT might say 'What about the time when Y, did you notice anything then?' We discuss this way of thinking about pedagogical helping in Chapter 9 (9.3.2 Scaffolding).

In work with groups of learners, each learner needs the opportunity to describe their experience, and so it is likely to be a better use of time available if this describing is done in small groups (see Chapter 9 – 9.3.1 The management of small-group work).

The types of experiences already used as starting points on the course so far

As with teaching pupils, if there is a choice of options, then ensuring that the full range are used as appropriate will support learners' continued engagement in the process.

Some examples of both types of experience and reasons why they might be chosen, are given below. As we said above, when choosing an appropriate starting-point experience ToTs need to believe that the ensuing discussion is likely to raise the kinds of issues that can be connected with the main needed (and therefore planned) input. The experience therefore ought to enable ToTs to 'get out' from the participants whatever is needed for them to be clear about why ToTs are 'putting in' what they have planned. Often this leaves ToTs with the choice of a number of options. For example, if they wanted to raise awareness of the need to develop the skill of noticing and planned an input on this (based perhaps on Mason 2003), then ToTs could choose as a starting-point experience a video, a demonstration activity or some micro-teaching which everyone would be asked to observe, after which different observations would be compared and reasons for the differences explored, explanations and implications discussed and so on. Which of these starting points you chose would depend on overall programme aims, the balance of the particular session you are planning and its position within the whole course (the horizontal threads), as well as more practical considerations such as the amount of time available and access to suitable resources/facilities. The table below outlines some types of starting-point experiences and some of the reasons we have chosen them.

Table 6

Type of experience	Reason for choosing as a Step 1 experience
A recalled real-world experience (e.g. of learning, teaching or of the subject to be taught) from before the session/course.	• Most/all participants will have had a real-world experience which will/can 'link' with the main planned 'input' or 'message' of the learning sequence. • Programme or ToT aims include 'convincing' participants of practical relevance of the programme aims and content. • Session or ToT aims include raising participants' awareness of 'differences' (of styles, of contexts, etc.).
In-session demonstration of teaching technique by ToT or experienced participant/expert skilled at the particular technique.	• Most/all participants will probably *not* have had experience of teaching or learning in this way. • Programme aims include developing the skills of noticing and this needs all participants to have experienced the 'same' thing.
Video of teaching, from same or different context.	• Programme or session aims include noticing skills development. • ToT/programme aims include

Type of experience	Reason for choosing as a Step 1 experience
	'convincing' participants that something is feasible in their context.
	• Session or programme aims include raising awareness of issues to do with classroom (and wider) cultures.
	• Programme or ToT aims include raising awareness of various teacher styles.
In-session game or fantasy activity.	• Most/all participants will probably *not* have had experience of teaching or learning in this way.
	• ToT aims require the provision of conditions for 'undermind insights' to emerge (for the development of KT).
	• Session plan requires inclusion of 'fun'.
Participants' 'micro-teaching'.	• Participants have got to a trying-out stage for a particular piece of KH development.
	• Participants need to develop confidence that 'they can do it'.
	• For noticing skill development.

We have only talked in detail here about selecting appropriate activities on which Step 1 will be based, because if this is not appropriate, the whole sequence will be less effective. For further details of all the subsequent steps see Chapter 3 in Part 1.

Back again to overall session planning

The draft session plans above were for a first session before we had actually met the participants. Planning of subsequent sessions is if anything slightly more complex in that it needs to take into account evidence from the previous session about where members of the group already are in their learning. Subsequent sessions often begin with a ToT saying something like 'In the last session you said/we found that . . . so in this session what I'm hoping we will do is . . . .' This thinking back in order to think forward requires the ToTs themselves to have noticed well how participants reacted, what they said, any evidence of their emotions and of course of learning. This is hard to do, especially as a beginner when new ToTs are far more focused on whether they look like a ToT, are doing all right, are being taken seriously, have remembered everything, have the timing 'right', etc. There are a number of ways to help yourself to notice. You could, for example, take the participants' emotional temperature during and/or at the end of a session by asking them to rate themselves on a 1–10 scale where 10 = happy and confident, and 1 = anxious and confused. You could also devise some way to get participants' views on what they learned or what they noticed. One simple method we often use (Malderez and Bodoczky 1999) is to ask each participant to note this down in five minutes on a small piece of paper at the end of each session or day. What do we do with all these notes? We read them, roughly analyse them, and try to see what they and what we recall noticing tells us about what participants feel they do and do not know, and how they are feeling, to inform our planning of the next session or series of sessions. In effect what we do here is use the experience of the session as the starting point (Step 1) for our own learning process.

Questions we might ask ourselves at the end of a session, using participants' notes and our own memories to help us answer them follow the five steps and might look something like this:

- What happened during the session – according to what I and others have noticed? In particular what seems to have been learned?
- So what do I think about that? How can I explain anything unexpected or unwanted?
- What do others think about things like that? How do others explain such events? (This is where ToTs may need to go off to the 'literature' or recall what they've read there, e.g. ideas in Part 1.)
- How do I now explain it, in the light of this?
- So what do I need to do in the next sessions to achieve my aims and how could I do it?

We see this process as a form of self-mentoring (see below for more) and it is in effect, a form of ongoing needs analysis.

Of course even when doing this we are bearing in mind our overall plan, because that was designed to help us achieve something by the end of the programme, but it is common that in each subsequent session tensions as regards timing emerge. The tension is between taking the time that the participants need as revealed by this ongoing needs analysis and going at the speed seemingly needed to achieve the overall programme aims by getting to the end of the plan. Especially designers, but also planners and some ToTs, are often very ambitious in terms of what is achievable in the time available. It is often understandable for designers, not only because they lack experience of ToTing, but also because they are often influenced by political pressure to be seen to 'get things done' quickly and by financial constraints. Where ToTs overestimate what it is realistic to achieve, this may be first because everyone tends to forget what it feels like to 'not know', and secondly because the very fact that they are ToTs probably means that they were fast learners and so, even when their memories are accurate, they will tend to underestimate how much time most teachers will need in order to learn. When worrying about these tensions of timing, new ToTs especially are likely to emphasize 'covering the programme plan'. Ultimately though, if the participants really cannot 'keep up', the design and/or planning stages have not accurately taken into account the learners' starting points or what it takes for a teacher to learn. In this case it is not the ToTs' fault, and in fact the programme might achieve more of its aims if *not* everything in the plan is covered. What is much more effective in the long term is if teachers leave a programme feeling they have been supported on the beginning stages of a learning journey, ideally equipped with some tools to continue that journey that they can actually use when they return to their classroom, even if not all sessions in the original programme plan have been completed. The other scenario when everything in the plan has been covered, but it has been too fast for the particular participants to cope, is likely to mean that they leave feeling bored, and that the programme was irrelevant and a waste of time. In such circumstances they are unlikely to feel willing and able to make the effort to do things differently in future, or to think about the ideas presented on the course again, or to attend any further programmes with enthusiasm and an open mind.

Unless, therefore, you are in an extremely controlled, autocratic top/down system that allows you no autonomy at all to decide how you will actually teach the programme (in which case next time you will need to try and influence design and/or planning stages to allow yourself more time and/or flexibility), don't worry about not doing everything that you might have originally planned, if you find that participants need more time. This does not represent selling them short, on the contrary, as we say above, it is the only way to proceed.

6.1.3 Handouts and hand-ins

As you will remember from your previous learning experiences as a teacher it is a widespread, taken-for-granted practice that course participants leave with text of some kind. On some courses this might be a prescribed textbook, but on the kinds of courses that ToTs are likely to be running such textbooks will not be available. Therefore, in part to meet participant expectations and in part for practical reasons, handouts are useful tools. So, once you have planned your session, the next part of concrete preparation is to decide what should go on the handouts and create these. Handouts come in many forms and we will discuss four basic forms here.

The first form is in effect the easiest to prepare and is a 'reading text'. This may be a part of a book or an article (with permission to reproduce obtained if necessary) and requires the ToT to have read it, thought why it is relevant, decided what they want participants to get out of it and devised a task to help them do so. This task or series of tasks may be one task given before the text, or the ToT might want to divide the text up into smaller chunks with tasks throughout the text. This latter form might be more appropriate for participants who are unfamiliar with doing much professional reading.

The second form of handout contains a summary of the session input. This requires you as a ToT to write out the main points of the input that you hope to be able to make (after the experience and 'getting out' phases).

A third form of handout contains the task instructions for activities in one or various phases of the session. This requires ToTs to think through what it is they want participants to do, and in what order. We gave an example of how this might look for one task above.

Another word here about the terms we are using. We talk about *tasks* here when we refer to in-class activities that have an endpoint, an outcome and a discussion element which require people, for example, to sort out ideas, agree on something defined, rank issues according to a set of criteria – that is to do something that has an end point and that is similar to the kind of thing people do in the real world. This differs from an *activity* which is much more of pedagogical classroom tool, and often has no obvious end. In an activity it is up to the ToT or the participants themselves to decide when to stop doing it and consider what can be learnt from it. A *game* is similar to many fun activities in some respects in that there is often not an endpoint, however it has rules for how it should be played. These definitions are ours written now and they overlap. It does not really matter too much what *you* call things, but is helpful to see the similarities and differences between the kinds of things you ask learners to do, because certain types of 'things you might ask learners to do' are more appropriate for some purposes and/or at some points in a session than others.

What we find helpful when thinking about handouts and task instructions is to think about the kinds of things that people can do in discussion tasks, and focusing on the verbs (agree – decide – rank) helps us in writing our task instructions, as well as helping us and the participants to decide when the task is over. Because a task has a natural endpoint and there is a need for learners to have a sense of success, it is inadvisable to stop their discussion before they have, e.g., come to an agreement. Obviously, if there are a number of groups, different groups will take different lengths of time to do so, and this is one reason that it is difficult to stick rigidly to timing in such sessions. Such situations need careful monitoring on the part of the ToT (see Chapter 9) and here it is useful to have a few quick small tasks (prepared, but probably not on the handout) to give to groups who have finished, while others complete the task.

Finally there are what we call 'gapped handouts', which as the name suggests have blank spaces on them intended for participants to use to make their own notes. For example you may have the title of the beginning experience on the handout followed by a space in which the participants can write down what they have noticed, learned from it, how the task was carried out, ideas about how they might use it themselves or anything else that strikes them and of which they want to keep a record. If using such a handout, time for completing it needs to be planned appropriately into the session, and perhaps some modelling of how this might be done will be needed in the early stages.

The four descriptions above could refer to separate handouts or ToTs might want to combine various of the above into a longer handout for a single session or day. We tend to try to keep handouts shorter rather than longer. This is for a number of reasons. First of all, if participants see that, for example, some of the planned tasks for the day have not been covered they may feel that this is their own or their ToT's fault, rather than an almost inevitable result of overestimating what can be learned (as opposed to covered or taught) in a given amount of time. Secondly, it is our experience that, if learners are to be able to use them after the course (one rationale for having them in the first place), they are not going to have time to reread a long text. A last reason is that a very long handout that has taken a lot of time to prepare may mean that the ToT becomes less flexible and responsive to what actually happens in the session. As with 'over planning' it is possible to 'over-prepare'.

The overall purpose of handouts is to be supportive of learning sequences. The type(s) of handout ToTs decide to prepare will depend on their particular purposes for creating the handouts. These purposes will also determine when in a particular session or course they decide actually to 'hand them out'. For example, thinking of the five steps, you might decide to have a gapped handout for Step 1 notes, followed by a task for Step 2 on one handout and a text for Step 3 on another one. If these are all on the same handout as that for Step 2, participants will, understandably, jump straight to the Step 3 text to find the 'right' answer.

Hand-ins

This is likely to be an unfamiliar term to most readers, but we increasingly like the notion of hand-ins. The content of hand-ins is produced by the participants rather than the ToT. An example might be the products of discussion activities that are written up by a ToT or a participant for distribution to the whole group as a record of the outcomes. If there is access to interactive technology, then these can be typed immediately onto the screen as people report back and, even better, if there is also a printer in the room it is possible to make the hand-in an instant handout, which often saves valuable evening preparation time on the ToT's part.

What is handed in and eventually becomes the content of a handout are participants' ideas. This has the advantage of more clearly demonstrating that everyone's ideas born of their experience are valuable and valued, as well as enabling the ToT to have a much better paper-based record of what was actually said for diagnostic purposes when planning future sessions.

A further type of hand-in that we have found useful is to ask participants within a given space of time, varying according to programme format, to think of their personal goals and/or the agreed group goals and go and search the programme library for something to read that might help them to further that goal and then provide a 1-page report under the headings What I read, why I read it, what I found and whether I would recommend it to group mates and why? These hand-ins are then turned into handouts and copies given to all participants via email or in hard copy.

6.1.4 Room arrangements

Above we have referred to the importance and potential effects on a session or programme of the kind of room you have and the flexibility of the furniture within it. Here we want to raise one or two other points to think about. Firstly of course ToTs need to think about the practicalities of how they will need the room to be laid out for the type of session that they have planned. They need to ask themselves about this from two points of view. The first is the practical: what will they be asking the participants to do first, and so how do they want the room arranged to begin with, and what rearrangement (if any) will be needed during the session and how will this be managed? The second, which is equally important, relates to what the layout implies: what messages about expected ToT/participant roles and relationships does the layout send, and are these what ToTs want/hope for? For example, rows of seats facing a ToT's table on a raised platform suggest a very traditional transmission-based approach in which the ToT is the 'knower' and the participants are passive receivers. These, as we hope is clear by now, are not roles that support our view of process of teacher learning.

One thing that is often ignored outside primary schools, mostly because in secondary and tertiary education learners and their teacher rarely have a permanent classroom in which they work over time, which is theirs and theirs alone, is thinking about the use of wall space. Many shorter teacher development courses on the other hand do have access to a single room for their duration, which potentially enables the wall space to be used for either ToT or participant-produced posters and displays. If these come from the ToT they may be used to reinforce main messages for or emerging from a particular session in visual as well as verbal ways (see Malderez and Bodoczky 1999). Those created by participants may be visual representations of the outcomes of groups' task-based work, which can be used in the final stage of a discussion when trying to synthesize the multiple perspectives generated. Types of posters participants on our previous courses have produced include:

- a typical learner
- the roles of a teacher
- a good teacher
- questions for textbook evaluation
- diagrams of the relationships between textbook teachers and learners
- elements of classroom culture
- elements of an ideal initial teacher education programme

In other words some tasks can have the creation of a poster as their outcome. This is, however, time-consuming, so we usually ask for posters only when dealing with issues that we particularly want the participants to remember or to which we will want to be able to refer throughout the programme.

Another possibility is a 'Yes but ... ' poster on which participants can note down at any time their individual thoughts regarding issues arising from any session or day, enabling the ToT to see participants' concerns and take these into account in planning and preparing the following sessions.

6.1.5 Ensuring all necessary day-to-day facilities are in place and functioning

It probably goes without saying here, that an obvious thing to remember is to check that you know how to use available facilities and whether they do actually work on the day. We have had many uncomfortable moments when we have forgotten to do this, or assumed that it had been done by someone else, and we still need to remind ourselves to follow our own advice!

Having said this, however, the presence and use of a lot of technology is not at all essential and is certainly not the major determinant of the potential effectiveness of a programme. If particular facilities that you have planned or expect to be able to use are not available, there are almost always ways to make up for their lack. We describe some of our experiences of doing this below.

We planned to use a video or DVD and then found that no playback facilities were available. We once again went back to our aims. Our purposes for choosing to use the video/DVD were:

- to show a technique in use in the participants' context, in order to demonstrate that it is feasible, and
- to help participants notice the key elements of the technique in action

We addressed the 'feasibility in the context' issue by inviting a teacher from the context who actually uses the technique to come and tell her story of using it and show her learners work as a result of using it. Another way, of course, could have been to take the participants to such a teacher's classroom, but this was less easy to organize.

In order to help participants notice and highlight important elements of the technique in use (the steps in the technique, teacher's language and movement at various steps, and the roles of teachers and learners at each step), which we needed to do as this was the beginning of a KH (know how) skill-development cycle, we resorted to demonstrating the technique ourselves with a few of the participants acting as learners in a kind of micro-teaching setting.

The table below sets out some other alternatives we have used in the absence of some commonly used facilities.

Table 7

Facility missing	What we have done instead
Whiteboard/blackboard	Flipchart, or brown wrapping paper on the wall.
OHT	Pre-prepared posters.
Tape recorder	Self reading tapescript as naturally as possible, perhaps with crude puppets, or other props (we've used hats) to support different voices.
Computer facilities (in training room or available anywhere in immediate context)	Take handwritten notes of group discussions and type/write them up in the evening + use of black/whiteboard. Abandon PowerPoint and pre-prepare posters.
Photocopier	Take essential handouts to be printed (reproduced) well in advance, and/or in-class use of posters and/or make time available for note-taking.

The points we are trying to make here are first that, if you are clear about your aims, you will find ways of achieving them even if the ideal facilities are not available. Secondly, if participants themselves do not have access to a range of facilities in their working context, part of our credibility as ToTs requires us to work in similar conditions. Finally, one of the most frequently heard complaints from teachers all over the world is that they cannot do a good job because they have not got the facilities. ToTs need to be able to demonstrate and remind participants that the most important facilities in any learning situation are the people (teachers and learners or ToTs and participants) and the contents of their heads.

6.2 Immediate 'preparation of self' for teaching

We entitled Part 1 of this book 'Preparing Yourself' and there is a sense in which the whole of this book is intended to help you 'prepare yourselves' for your practices as a ToT, and a quick reread or skim through before a programme begins might be helpful. In addition, if you have been fortunate enough to have been involved in the design and planning stages of the programme on which you are working, you will have been 'preparing yourself' for quite some time. The necessary reading of resources will also have helped you prepare yourself in terms of developing your confidence in your understanding of the KA aspects of the programme that you hope to be able to provide as input. There is, though, one final and crucial part of 'preparation of self' which can support your actual teaching or implementation of your session plans, and this is what we deal with here.

There will always be things ToTs do and say during sessions which are not formally pre-planned or scripted. In order to try and ensure that these are helpful for our participants' learning we like to prepare ourselves just before the session when all the concrete preparation is finished by looking carefully at each element of the session plan and asking ourselves three questions: Why? How? and What if?

The first question we ask is 'Why?' Why am I asking participants to do this, why have I planned this? We try to think of three kinds of answers:

- A contextual answer – e.g. because there has been a reform in which participants are being expected to deal differently with their textbooks
- A 'theoretical' answer relating to teacher learning – e.g. 'Because I need first to give them an experience or help them to remember an experience'
- An answer relating to these particular participants – e.g. 'Because participants said in reply to my pre-course letter that . . . ', or 'Because in the last session we had not fully completed . . . /someone said . . . '

It is this final answer relating to our particular participants that we find particularly useful in class when giving participants an all-important purpose for what we are asking them to do, e.g. 'You said last session that. . . . So now we are going to explore that . . . Let's start by . . . '

The second question we ask ourselves when looking at each stage of the session plan is 'How?' This does not relate to the exact activity or task which we have already decided (although we have made some last-minute changes of task/activity at this stage too), but instead to 'How am I going to be'? This requires us to imagine ourselves actually in the room, setting up, monitoring, giving instructions, moving round the room and so on, bearing in mind our specific session aims, more general programme aims and our overall approach, and to consider the various ways we could do these things. As we imagine, we 'talk' to ourselves, for example: 'So then they are discussing, and I'll stand here ... oh no, they could think I don't trust them to get on alone ... Perhaps I'll go and sit where I'm not very visible.... But what about checking they have understood the task ... I'd better monitor for that first part and then go there ... '

The final question we ask ourselves for each element of the plan as well as the plan overall is 'What if ... ?' In considering as many possible scenarios as we can we think of our particular participants and what we know of them. Here we are trying to imagine anything that might 'go wrong' or, more accurately, make a difference to our plan (for example in terms of timing), or participants' learning (for example finding a task difficult), in order to prepare ourselves to respond during the session in helpful and appropriate ways. This may lead us to add extra stars (items to possibly omit) to our plan, or to note ideas for tasks for early finishers, or to imagine forms of word to reassure or support particular participants, as well as how to respond to 'Yes, buts ... ', or pre-empt them.

The result of this preparation of self is not that things happen exactly as you imagine them even then, but rather that through this thinking and imagining process you have considered a range of scenarios. This makes it more likely that an appropriate response will pop into your head when you need it, as the unpredictable and messy events of any session unfold.

You may find this difficult to do to begin with, so here are a couple of ways we have used to help ourselves to do it better/more easily/quickly.

For the 'How?' question above one way to think of alternative ways of doing things (so that you can then picture yourself doing them) could be by describing something you actually did (e.g. I wrote on the blackboard) and then thinking about possible substitutions for each word in the sentence, imagining what the effects would have been if the changed sentence had in fact been a true description of what happened. For example:

- *A participant* wrote on the backboard
- I *stuck a* ... on the blackboard
- I wrote on the *poster*

At each substitution we ask ourselves questions like:

- Is this something I have ever done?
- Could I do it?
- What sort of effect would it have?
- Would it be helpful?

This process (particularly fun to do with a colleague!) has helped us be creative, more imaginative and develop – and use – new alternatives.

Thinking of 'What if?' questions, you will probably find that with more experience you develop more 'What ifs', if only because you (like us) have experienced more 'disasters' and so become more able to imagine a range of 'What ifs' that might stop the session going exactly according to plan. Other ways you might be helped to speed up this process is by remembering how you felt as a participant on similar programmes, or by carefully noticing the reactions of particular 'problematic' participants (the one who *always* says 'Yes, but ... ', the one who often seems disengaged, the one who seems to 'finish' before everyone else, the one who often seems to have misunderstood what to do/what it is you or others are trying to say ... and so on).

Sometimes as a result of this noticing you may in fact decide that you need to do more than just make a minor adjustment to how you behave or what you say in a session. For example, you may identify a general need to pay more attention to, or even devote some more extensive time to developing your own skills in, for example, managing small-group work or active listening (see Part 3).

The planning and preparation stages above have all assumed that a ToT would be working with a group of teachers. However, for a number of reasons, there is now increasing recognition of the importance of working one-to-one with teachers in their real classrooms. These reasons include: the growing understanding of what learning to be a teacher involves; ideas about situated learning and that learners need to be where they will actually have to do things if they are to learn how to do them; and ideas about reflective practice.

Chapter 7

Working one-to-one

Designers and planners of our imaginary programme who have an ultimate goal that includes reflective practice and an awareness of socio-cultural understandings of teacher learning, would ideally have budgeted for the preparation and use of school-based ToTs to support participants as they worked in their own environments both in the four-week period between blocks as well as subsequently. In much of the current literature these school-based ToTs may be referred to as mentors, although, as with many of these role-based titles, what different people mean by the term 'mentor' is becoming increasingly diverse. Our view of what a mentor is, what mentoring is and how you might engage in one-to-one work, building on that presented in Malderez and Bodoczky 1999, is discussed here. Before we begin, a reminder that for us mentoring, like all ToTs' work, is based on the sorts of understandings of the teacher-learning process presented in Part 1.

7.1 Mentors and mentoring

Think back to when you were learning to teach. Ask yourself the following questions:

- How did you learn the culture, the particular rules and ways of doing things of the school that you first worked in? Did anyone tell you things before you needed them or only after you had got something wrong? Were you left to 'pick it up' by yourself?
- Beginning teaching is often an emotional experience. Was there anyone to provide a shoulder to cry on or a listening ear?
- Was there anyone who you remember as being particularly helpful for your teaching by, for example, making suggestions or lending you materials or handouts, or being willing to answer your queries?
- How did you feel when you were, or felt you were (as everyone initially does) making a mess of things in your classroom? Did you know what to do or where to turn?
- Was there anyone you admired and decided to try to be like?

Some of you may be able to picture particular people or even a single person who did some or all of these things for you when you first started teaching. In many ways, whether formally appointed or not that person was informally your mentor or those people were collectively performing mentoring roles. Mentoring itself is not new, but it is only recently that we have realized how important it is in teacher learning. Its importance lies in the fact that the classroom is the only site where the learner teacher can integrate the three kinds of knowledge. If this integration does not occur in the classroom, much of what has been taught on initial or in-service teacher-education programmes will be lost. For many, the process of integrating their knowledge often needs real support over time from some sort of mentoring figure(s) and a lack of appropriate support is one of the reasons, together with inappropriate programme design and planning, that teacher-education programmes of all kinds so often seem to have little or no real impact on participants' teaching.

There are, however, a number of clear reasons why this one-to-one support is so rare. First it is expensive, because it requires a mentor teacher to have time to spend with each mentee. This is time which will not be spent teaching a class and so it has implications for school budgets. In addition, teachers who become mentors need considerable time to prepare for their new roles and practice, which adds further costs. Whereas ToTs working with a group can draw on many of the skills that they use in the classroom (assuming that they adapt their teaching to the needs of their learners), supporting an individual teacher's learning one-to-one requires a seemingly different set of skills.

One way of thinking about what it means to be a mentor is to think about some mentor roles.

Acculturator

The first role that may be relevant, especially for new teachers is for the mentor to be responsible for helping the newcomer to the school understand the culture they are entering. This needs time (starting on Day 1 or soon after, and continuing for as long as necessary) and requires the mentor to do a range of things such as introduce the mentee to everyone; show them round the school; tell them about rules and expectations from formal procedures (what registration details to take) to less formal but nonetheless institutionalized rituals such as which chair belongs to whom in the staff room.

Model

In remembering who helped you when you first became a teacher you may remember somebody as your role model. Modelling is an important thing for mentors to do. This is less about modelling ways of teaching to be copied and more about modelling enthusiasm for learning, membership of professional groups, attitudes to peers, learners and parents, and so on.

Support

Another important role as your memories may have reminded you is that of being a shoulder to cry on or a listening ear. To make this possible a mentor needs to develop a close and trusting relationship with their mentee and then make themselves available for such personal encounters. This may involve physical proximity (for example, moving desk next to mentee or having an adjacent room and leaving the door open and making it clear that you are happy to be approached and talked to at more or less any time, or giving your home phone number) and will certainly involve being willing to make that time available. Sometimes in this support role the best thing a mentor can do for a stressed mentee is to offer to do something practical like get the photocopying done.

Sponsor

The role of the mentor includes the assumption that the mentor will use whatever power they do have in support of the mentee (for example, interceding on your mentee's behalf in a school budget meeting to obtain materials that you know your mentee would appreciate).

In the business world this kind of behaviour is called 'sponsoring' and may involve, for example, introducing a mentee to the 'right people'. For learning teaching, with a 'professional teacher' as the ultimate goal, this might mean taking a mentee with you to a professional conference.

Educator

Finally and crucially, the mentor has a role in more directly supporting their mentee's learning of classroom teaching by helping the integration of the various types of knowledge the mentee has, as well as expanding these. Here, the main activities that a mentor needs to engage in to complete this aspect of their role are purposeful listening and talking. We expand on what we mean by this below.

In a typical scenario, a mentor will want to get the mentee to talk about what is going on in their classroom in order to support their learning. The mentor might start with a 'How's it going?' and follow this up with 'So tell me about your last lesson'. At this point the mentor is actively listening and using what they hear to understand a number of things about the way the mentee thinks. For example there may be clues in what the mentee does and does not talk about as to the kinds of concerns that are preoccupying them, which many have associated with stages of teacher development.

Those in the early stages of their development as teachers tend to be concerned mostly with themselves and the content of the talk is likely to include a lot of references to what the mentee did or said or forgot or was worried about in the lesson but fewer references to what the learners did or seemed to be feeling and even fewer, if any, about any evidence that the learners were learning. This is not just a feature of novice teachers' talk. There are a number of conditions in which even people who have been teaching for some years may be at this stage. For some people it will be because they have never moved on from this stage, and we tend to think this occurs in cases where initial teacher preparation has focused almost exclusively on 'training' appropriate teacher behaviour and where being a good teacher is assessed by whether the teacher does things 'correctly'. For others it will be a result of having to change their teaching behaviour for some reason, and so starting a new learning process.

> The above stages are as true for learning to be a ToT as they are for learning to be a schoolteacher. However experienced any ToT is, when they start teaching a new group, they will be concerned about how learners will see them and whether they will be accepted and respected as a ToT. This concern, and apparent 'regression' to an earlier stage of professional development, can be noticeable when ToTs work with new groups on repeat courses, but is particularly noticeable when they are teaching a totally new group (for example moving from being a teacher to a ToT, or moving from teaching learners of one kind to another, or teaching a similar course to similar people using a different approach).

Going back to a mentor listening to a teacher; the teacher when describing what happened in the lesson may refer less to anything they do or think they did, and more to the reactions and behaviours of learners. They may talk about specific pupils or pupils in general, what they did, whether or not they seemed to be working, specific examples of misbehaviour, evidence of interest, but may not make reference to student learning as such. On hearing such talk a mentor might diagnose that a teacher, with that group at least, has arrived at a stage where they can focus on the pupils, but they do not yet seem to be overtly concerned with whether or not the pupils were learning or had in fact learned anything. *How* the teachers talk, as much as what they say, can be used to gauge a more precise focus for ensuing work. Again referring to this latter teacher, if s/he seemed upset by some aspect of pupil behaviour it would seem logical to deal with this in relation both to what the teacher might do next time so as not to get upset, and in relation to types of pupil behaviour that promote learning (many teachers are upset when pupils talk in class, yet it is known that many learners need to talk to learn, and teacher-learners in particular need such opportunities). By choosing this focus, the mentor will be addressing what the mentee is ready to learn, while also gradually trying to focus on learning, since what matters about what happens in a classroom is the extent to which it does or does not promote learning.

How the mentor conducts the discussion matters in many ways, and we will suggest a structure for this kind of discussion in which the mentor, while listening carefully, can diagnose and guide in ways that not only move the teacher on to broader concerns than their own or their pupils' behaviours but also help the mentee integrate the available knowledges they have. Again we return to the five steps (see Part 1) which suggest a rough structure for these kinds of conversations.

Five steps for post-lesson discussions in mentoring

In a situation where a mentee is *already* skilled at learning from experience, what a mentor needs to do after a particular experience of teaching (observed or not) is as follows:

1. **Listen** *actively* (while the mentee describes what they noticed) and, if the class has been observed by the mentor, and when invited to do so by the mentee, *share* what they noticed
2. **Listen** *actively* (while the mentee explores as many explanations/ interpretations of what they noticed as they can) and, when invited, *add* any other possible explanations
3. **Listen** *actively* (while the mentee recalls what others have said or written about the issues raised) and, possibly and if different, *share* what they know about what others say or have written
4. **Listen** *actively* (while the mentee considers these different perspectives, and decides which explanation is most likely and why) and possibly, when invited, *clarify* the logic of the argument
5. **Listen** *actively* (while the mentee, based on their analysis of the experience described in 1, makes decisions and concrete plans about what to do next for their own as well as their pupils' learning) and possibly, *share* what they know about what others do when faced with similar situations, and/or *support* the concrete planning process

We said that the two main things that a mentor actually has to do in their supporting the learning of teaching role is to listen and talk in informed and structured ways. (Many when asked what mentors do will say 'Observe and give feedback'. We however believe that this process is more central to assessing teaching than it is to mentoring/supporting teacher learning, and there is a sense in which the main purpose of mentoring rather than to 'give' anything, is to help learners to discover and make links for themselves – see Part 3, 9.3.2 Scaffolding). In mentoring (in contrast to 'training' aspects of KH, or to assessing teaching, see Part 4), observing lessons is not always needed, and indeed it is sometimes best for a mentor not to have observed a lesson. When the mentor has not observed the lesson being discussed it makes the question 'Tell me what happened' a genuine one and creates a real reason for the mentee to describe what they noticed in as full a way as possible in order to help the mentor imagine what the lesson was like. In addition, not observing the lesson can make the mentee less nervous than they would generally be (partly because lesson observation is and has been associated with assessment). It can also allow the mentee to choose whether to disclose any real 'disasters' at early stages of the mentor–mentee relationship. Although observation is not necessary, it can be helpful as long as the mentor uses the occasion to gather observation data which can be fed into an initial describing what happened (Step 1) phase of the discussion. We say *can* be useful because the skill of observing and recording such data is complex and inept observations, in our experience, can do more harm than good. The ideal scenario is one in which the mentee invites the mentor into the classroom to be another pair of eyes, to notice for them a particular phenomenon relating to something that they are working on developing. This will only occur in a genuinely non-judgemental partnership and when the mentee has seen the value of the process they are engaged in and developed trust in the mentor.

Mentoring processes aim at achieving such positive partnerships.

7.2 Mentoring: the design stage

If the use of mentors is going to be part of any planned programme to support teacher learning, it needs to be part of the design stage from the outset. As with teacher education programmes many mentor schemes that have been established have not had the hoped-for effects. This again, as with teacher-education schemes, can be the result of insufficient and/or inappropriate mentor preparation, insufficient money (and so time), and/or insufficient attention having been paid to contextual factors at both societal and institutional levels.

Going back to our imaginary programme above, it was assumed at the design stage that for the first cohort the ToTs would go into schools during the four-week inter-block period, to act as mentors to the participants as they tried to work on using their textbook more responsively. In addition, this first cohort were given a further week of mentor training (to be followed up with further opportunities for mentoring development) to prepare them in turn to act as mentors for future cohorts. The initial-needs analysis undertaken for the programme as a whole will help define the contribution that mentoring is expected to make to achieving the aims of the programme.

Cascade models (such as the one described above) have often been disappointing in their impact and effectiveness. This can in large measure (we believe) be explained because what was cascaded was only the 'content' of the course (the KA, what can be known about), which is likely to have been less and less appropriately 'transmitted' as the cascade continued. However, if what is cascaded is an investigation–articulation, looking back to look forward, 'swinging', five-step approach to learning, then this is likely, by definition, to be relevant to learners at any level of the cascade. In such 'new style' cascades of provision, mentors have a critical role to play.

7.3 Mentoring: the planning stage

So how would you plan as a mentor (who, of course, is basically a ToT working one-to-one)? In some contexts the starting point would be helping the mentee become familiar with the school – an induction phase. This will obviously not be necessary in our imaginary context, but even here you will need to begin the mentoring process (as the ToTs working with groups did above) by establishing norms, setting goals and building a (more) trusting relationship. This may mean making explicit when you will be free to spend time with the teacher and what sorts of support you feel able to offer. These may include, for example: help in thinking about student needs, analysing the textbook and lesson planning, discussing what happened as a result of the lesson plan) and helping the mentee collect evidence about the effects of using the textbook more flexibly so that they can return to the second block of the programme with ideas to contribute to the discussions of people's experiences. Planning at this point involves planning to state explicitly, that *this is what I see I might be able to do to support you, and this is when and where and for how long I suggest we meet.* Because of the need for a mentor to diagnose mentee needs as they unfold, further detailed planning is probably impossible at this stage.

7.4 Mentoring: concrete preparation

In such a programme, mentor concrete preparation might involve ensuring that they (mentor and mentee) will have access to suitable support materials, such as the teachers' book for the coursebook in use (if available), a range of other text-books, supplementary materials, stationery and facilities for creating materials, and so on.

You will also need to use your knowledge of your school (or the school where the mentee works), its culture and the relationships within it, to predict any particular circumstances that might impact on the effectiveness of your mentoring. There are three main things to think about: time (and timetabling), atmosphere and space.

Time/timetabling

Have you and your mentee been allocated enough time for the mentoring process? If not, can you at this stage negotiate any more? How will you deal with this? Are timetabling arrangements suitable for both you and the mentee to have the necessary time together? Could they be better arranged?

Atmosphere

Is the institutional atmosphere supportive of mentoring in general and of the purpose of this particular mentoring process? For example, if the head teacher is particularly authoritarian and conservative or from a subject discipline with a different associated methodology, there may be little support for, or even suspicion of, what you and your mentee are trying to do. Recognizing this before you start can help you think of ways you might be able to help your head teacher understand what you are hoping to achieve and why (see 'whys' above) before the mentoring begins, or at least, 'protect' your mentee during the process. Or, you may decide, as you think about your/the school, that some members of staff who have authority in the school because of age, years of experience and or position, might find it strange or inappropriate that parts of the staffroom are taken up with, for example, scissors, cardboard and glue. Can you perhaps either explain (in ways that are convincing) beforehand, or perhaps even obtain/commandeer a different space for such activities?

Space

In respect of 'space', what about your need to be 'available'? Is your room/space in the staffroom close to that of your mentee? Could you arrange for it to be so if it is not now? Will you and your mentee have a private space to meet and talk?

'Preparation of self' for mentors, as for ToTs who work with groups of teachers, will have begun during as many of those earlier stages as designers and planners of the overall programme have involved them in. (And it is perhaps evident that we see as an ideal scenario that all ToTs, those working with groups as well as with teachers one-to-one if different, *are* involved in all earlier stages). However, at the immediate pre-mentoring phases, 'preparation of self' can involve mentors in re-familiarizing themselves with what it is that the mentee has to learn, and through ToT literature (including perhaps this book) what their part in helping the mentee learn it might be. In doing this it will again be helpful to remember what it felt like to not know or be able to do what they are expected to help the mentee learn, as well as to think through and note what they want to achieve in the first meeting. As with ToTs working with groups, this 'first meeting plan' can be checked through asking the 'Whys, the 'Hows' and the 'What ifs'. (For more on the skills and practices of ToTs working one-to-one, see Part 3)

> Mentor's notes for a first meeting with a mentee on the above programme could look like this:
>
> *Aims* To establish a working relationship
>
> To find out my mentee's attitude to course expectations
>
> To find out my mentee's current concerns
>
> To plan a focus for next steps together and agree the time of the next meeting
>
> - So how are you enjoying the programme so far?
> - What do you see us doing together over the next 4 weeks?
> - So which class are you thinking of using for the textbook adaptation work?
> - What are the children like? What difficulties do they have? What do they need/want/like most?
> - Where do we go from here? What would it be useful for you to do next? What do you see my role as being in helping you do it?
> - When shall we next meet?

You will note that the 'parts' of the discussion have been signalled by 'questions' which we find a helpful mentoring form of 'session planning'. As we noted above, the main things that mentors do is listen, and preparing actual questions, designed to prompt mentee articulation and achieve particular purposes for particular people at particular stages of learning, is a means of both 'session planning' and 'preparation of self'.

> Some 'why, how, what if' thinking for a mentor with regard to the first question (phase of the session) above might include:

WHY

- They are in the middle of a course and knowing how they are feeling about it will affect the way that I approach my mentoring.
- Because I need to establish a way of working, I need a collegial way of working in which I am a listener as much as/rather than a talker. By encouraging them to talk first I am modelling this.

HOW

- I need to listen actively, behind the words, and watch out for signs of confusion, scepticism or distress, or enthusiasm, confidence or interest.

WHAT IF

- What if the mentee is totally fed up with the programme and is not at all convinced that doing anything different with the textbook is necessary or useful?
- I could try to share how I used to think like that but what an amazing difference it made when I did start thinking about how I could match the textbook better to my learners' real needs.
- I need to be careful not to make the trainee defensive. Suggest s/he can have a go and if it makes no difference I will have to be very careful to make sure we spend enough time discovering learner's needs and evaluating the outcome of any adaptations made so that s/he does make and notice a difference.

Conclusion

In Part 2 we have thought about the practices of designing, planning and preparing for ToTs working with groups of teachers as well as one-to-one, within the broad investigation–articulation approach on which this book is based. We believe that what has been said here is relevant to processes which will help achieve all the ultimate goals of teacher learning, since even a programme aiming to produce technicist teachers will need to enable them to articulate the ideas that they think lie behind a particular syllabus/set of materials. Since we cannot work with you as readers directly on implementing ideas in your actual teaching, Part 3 has two broad aims. First it suggests ways in which you (and your colleagues) can help yourselves develop your in-session teaching skills, and secondly, through examples aims to provide further practical suggestions. If you have never taught teachers before, perhaps the best advice we can offer is the advice we received from a colleague when first teaching teachers, which was 'just listen'.

Materials and activities used in examples in Part 2

Example Pre-course Letter aiming to assess a particular group of participants' subjective understanding of their lacks and wants (in terms of target and process needs) for use in planning (see Chapter 6, concrete preparation):

Dear _____ [participant's name],

We look forward to meeting and working with you on _____ [date, time, place] for the start of the programme entitled: *Using your textbook more effectively to support your learners' learning.*

We would like to ask you to bring the (or a) textbook you frequently use with you to the programme.

In addition, to help us plan the programme in a way which will be most useful to you and meet your expectations, we would be very grateful if you could let us have your responses to the questions set out below. When you have written your answers (notes are fine), please send them back to us in the stamped, addressed envelope enclosed. Alternatively, if it is more convenient, we would be happy to receive your answers by email. Our addresses are given below.

With very best wishes,

[(ToTs) + contact details]

---

1. Do you have any novel ways of using the textbook that you have devised to meet your learners' needs? If so, please briefly describe them here.

2. Do you have any difficulties using the textbook you currently have with your pupils? If so what are they?

3. What do you hope to achieve through (this programme? What do you hope to be able to do better or to do differently as a result of this programme?

4. What do you hope the programme will be like? What do you expect from the ToT(s), and fellow participants? How do you like to learn?

Question 1 above aims to find out how flexible the particular participants might already be in their textbook use. The kinds of answers that can be received might vary from descriptions of times when they have asked the pupils to put the books away or close the textbook, to more complex descriptions of adaptations or supplementations. In the former case knowing this will help us to remind participants that they are already making some flexible choices about how and/or when they use their textbook. In the latter case, if there are many responses of this kind it suggests that there was a problem in the needs analysis at the design stage. We would then think 'Help!' and have to think about how to adapt our planning so that we are not 'teaching' participants things that they can already do. If there are only one or two responses like this, we would not revise our plan, but finding out who these people are will be an important early task for us on the programme, so that we can make sure that their experience and expertise is used as fully as possible. In particular they will provide extremely useful evidence that what is being proposed is feasible in the context.

Responses to question 2 will enable ToTs to find out what participants already know they need to know, as well as to infer, from what they have not written about, what they will need to be made aware of before they can be expected to see the relevance of any planned learning. If the difficulties mentioned are common across the group of participants it would make sense to ensure that the programme addresses these early on.

The simple fact of asking question 3 encourages participants to begin thinking about their own personal goals for the programme, and the ease or otherwise with which participants seem to have been able to respond to this question may also reveal something about previous course experiences that participants have had. For example, if participants seem to have found answering this question difficult (and you can judge this because answers give few precise goals or they are expressed in terms of the title of the course), this might suggest that previous experience as participants on in-service programmes has been one in which they were not encouraged to truly participate and so develop their own goals, but rather only to 'receive' whatever input the ToTs had chosen.

> As we write the word 'participate' above, we are reminded that one of the things we want to make clear in this book is that the approach we advocate for teacher learning would be one that might otherwise be included under 'participatory approaches'.

Answers to question 4 allow ToTs to become clearer about participants' expectations as regards the process of the course. Again responses may range from 'to be told how to do it', or 'to share experiences and discuss ideas with other participants', to 'to have fun', or 'to make new friends'. Understanding participants' expectations of the process, especially if what you hope to do is very different from their expectations, will influence, for example, your decisions about how much training in small-group work participants will need (see Part 3), or whether the initial session plan may need to include a phase in which you 'blind them with science' by giving them formal input on why they will not be getting formal input all the time!

Name game

We will give a brief description of this 'fun' activity here (for fuller details see Malderez and Bodoczky 1999).

- All group members including the ToT(s) stand in a circle.
- Participants are told that the aim of the activity is for everyone to learn everyone else's name (and perhaps given some further rationale: 'We are going to be working very closely together and so we need to get know each other, and to do this we need to know each other's names').
- In the first phase participants say their name as they throw a ball (soft toy, beanbag, screwed up piece of paper) randomly to somebody else in the circle.
- When everyone has had at least one chance to hear everyone else's name, the rules of the game change and it is the receiver of the ball who now says the name of the thrower. This can cause consternation at first and 'cheating' is allowed/positively encouraged (if the receiver can't remember the name of the thrower, anyone standing close who does can whisper it – the ToT may need to model this 'cheating' in a jokey way first).
- As soon as the ToT at least feels they can name everyone in the group, the activity is stopped and the ToT shows off by doing so!
- Participants are not asked to show publicly how many names they can remember, but rather to think about those names they can't remember and to make an effort to learn them during the course of the first day.

Get a new chair

Again full details of this game can be found in Malderez and Bodoczky 1999.

- All participants, but not the ToT, are seated on chairs arranged as a circle.
- There is no spare chair in this circle for the ToT.
- Participants know that the aim of the game is to get a new chair, and that the ToT also wants a chair, so someone in the group will not be successful. To get the new chair they will have to move, but there are certain conditions under which they can and cannot move.
- They can only move when they hear their 'names', but they will be given new 'names'.
- The ToT then goes round the circle labelling each member with one of four or five terms relevant to the course purpose. For example here we might use *'select'*, *adapt'*, *'omit'*, *'supplement'*, since all of these relate to ways of using textbooks more flexibly.
- Participants move only when they hear their label called out by the person standing in the centre. For the first round this is the ToT.
- If the person standing in the centre wants everyone to move, they can call out *'textbook'*.
- Participants play the game according to two other rules. There are that they may not return to sit on the chair that they started from, nor – when *textbook*

is called – on either of the chairs immediately adjacent to their original position.

- Participants are offered the chance to take off their shoes if they wish and also reminded to be careful since there will a large number of people running in different directions in a fairly small space.

The game is played for several rounds during which a number of different course participants will find themselves stranded in the centre without a chair.

After this the ToT pauses the game and adds an additional task which is to notice the strategies that are being used by group members to achieve their goal (find a new chair to sit on). The game continues for a few more rounds.

After the game the ToT joins the circle and elicits what strategies group members have noticed. People commonly mention: listening carefully, watching when people move, deciding to go sideways not across, aiming for one chair and needing to change direction because circumstances changed, putting in a lot of energy.

The ToT can then ask if they can see any connections between what they have said and learning. The point is made that the ToT hopes that all members will listen carefully, have a goal, be ready to be flexible about the goal if conditions on their 'learning journey' change, recognize that other people have different goals and so different people might want/need to be going in different directions, and be careful that their focus on their own goal does not get in the way of other people being able to reach theirs.

As a continuation from the Get a new chair game, participants are told that they will be guided through an activity to develop individual and group goals so that the ToT has a better idea of which 'chairs to put out' on the course.

For this they will need to be in groups, and so the purpose of the next small task is to enable small groups to be formed.

Experience line-up

- Participants are asked to line up in a single line (which need not be straight if the room does not allow it to be) according to the number of years of teaching experience each has.
- Participants spend a few minutes asking each other about their experience and arranging themselves accordingly.
- Before counting off a number (4–5) of participants to form small groups, which will then disperse to tables round the room, the ToT quickly adds up the total number of years' experience of all the participants and, as said previously, makes the point that this (huge) amount of experience will be invaluable for the course process.

Goal setting

- Although sitting in small groups, participants are asked to spend a few minutes individually making notes of what they would like to achieve by the end of the programme.

- A group task is then given which asks individuals to take turns to tell other group members about their individual goals, after which the group is required to agree on a maximum of goals (we usually use either three or four).
- A spokesperson from each group (see Part 3, 9.3.1 The management of small-group work) reads out their small-group goals to the whole group.
- The synthesized goals from all of the small groups become a hand-in representing the whole-group goals, 'the chairs'.
- Everyone has the chance to have a copy of these. They can be referred to at the end of the programme so that participants can identify the opportunities there have been on the programme to achieve the goals and the extent to which they have made best use of the opportunities and actually achieved the goals.

ToTs will also need to check to what extent they have already planned to provide opportunities for participants to meet the particular goals that have been developed, and where necessary think about how they can fit such opportunities into the programme. This way of organizing tasks (from individual thinking to small-group work, to whole-group work) is called a 'pyramid discussion' format and is an extremely useful way of organizing the work around many tasks.

References

Berry, R. S. Y. (2003) English language teaching and learning in mainland China: a comparison of the intentions of the English language curriculum reform and the real-life teaching and learning situation in the English classroom. *Hong Kong Institute of Education NAS Newsletter* 4 3–6)

Hadfield, J. (1992) *Classroom Dynamics.* Oxford: Oxford University Press

Malderez, A. and Bodoczky, C. (1999) *Mentor Courses: A resource book for Trainer Trainers.* Cambridge: Cambridge University Press

Mason, J. (2002) *Researching your own practice: The discipline of noticing.* London: Routledge Falmer

Further reading

Needs analysis/course design

For references to needs and wants analysis we have always drawn on our own discipline which has a long-standing, large and complex literature:

Graves, K. (1997) *Teachers as Course Developers.* Cambridge: Cambridge University Press, Chapter 2 provides a framework within which to consider course development processes, as do the first six chapters of Graves, K. (2000) *Designing*

Language Courses. Boston: Heinle & Heinle. When looking at either of these you will need to 'translate' the references to language teaching to ToTing.

One common model for designing large scale ToTing is known as a Cascade model. You will find reference to this in journals of educational change, educational development and educational management. Two articles that look at examples of such cascade programmes in action and note some of the design implications that are likely to determine whether the supposed benefits of such models actually occur are:

Hayes, D. (2000) Cascade training and teachers' professional development. *English Language Teaching Journal* 54(2), 135–45

Wedell, M. (2005) Cascading training down into the classroom: the need for parallel planning. *International Journal of Educational Development* 25(6), 637–51

Planning

There is little written in this area and this relates to initial teacher preparation. This perhaps reflects the recentness of the shift from theory–application to investigation–articulation approaches and/or an assumption that a ToT can still plan exactly as they would if they were teaching in school and/or because the existence of a contextually taken-for-granted way (often a 'form' to be filled in) of making the results of the planning process public.

Concrete preparation

Resources for session ideas will mainly include ideas from our own discipline. Again you may need to 'adjust' these if you are ToTing with teachers of subjects other than language. However you will find many of these address aspects of general pedagogic knowledge (in Shulman's terms) and so are relevant to all teachers. In addition because the ultimate aim of language teaching is to enable learners to acquire the complex open skill of language use, many of these ideas are very relevant to ToTing of all kinds. Titles on our shelves which we refer to frequently include:

Woodward, T. (2004) *Ways of working with teachers: Principled recipes for the core tasks of teacher training, teacher education and mentoring*. Broadstairs: Tessa Woodward publications

Some of her other titles are also well worth consulting. They include:

Loop input (1988) Canterbury: Pilgrims Publications

Models and metaphors in language teacher training (1991) Cambridge: Cambridge University Press)

James, P. (2001) *Teachers in action: Tasks for in-service language teacher education and development*. Cambridge: Cambridge University Press

Freeman, D. and Cornwell, S. (Eds) (1993) *New ways in teacher education*. Alexandria VA: TESOL

Fanselow, J. F. (1992) *Contrasting conversations: Activities for exploring our beliefs and teaching practices*. White Plains, NY: Longman

Head, K. and Taylor, P. (1997) *Readings in teacher development*. Oxford: Heinemann

Farrell, T. S. C. (2004) *Reflective practice in action: Eighty reflection breaks for busy teachers.* Thousand Oaks, CA: Corwin Press

Malderez and Bodoczky (1999). Although this is a resource book for those teaching ToTs who work one-to-one (mentors), with some adaptation many of the ideas can be used in planning to teach teachers. A couple of these are referred to specifically in this and other sections.

Mentoring

This, like reflective practice, means different things to different people in different places. It has moved from the business world to initial teacher preparation and later to in-service support (like the UK induction year). If looking at literature about mentoring you therefore need to look carefully at what the writers mean by the term, since not all of them will mean one-to-one ToTing of the kind described in this book.

If you have looked at Malderez and Bodoczky (1999) for ideas, you could now look at Chapter 1, for a discussion of a view of the basic concepts of mentoring. Tomlinson (1995) was also mentioned in Part 1.

Edwards, A. and Collison, J. (1996) *Mentoring and developing practice in primary schools.* Buckingham: Open University Press

This is situated firmly within socio-cultural approaches to teacher education and their concept of mentoring is quite close to ours of one-to-one ToTing. They use data from research to underline the fact that one-to-one ToTing is not an instinctive activity, and that there are new skills and knowledge which need to be learnt.

An early book which we have found helpful is

McIntyre, D., Hagger, H. and Wilkin, M. (1993) *Mentoring: Perspectives on school-based teacher education.* London: Kogan Page

This contains a number of chapters relevant to one-to-one ToTing.

Journals

Some of those mentioned in Part 1 will contain articles relevant to the topics discussed here. Another one we would like to recommend is the *Teacher Trainer*, (Canterbury: Pilgrims Publications.) Although this is focused on teaching language teachers, many of its extremely practical articles are more widely relevant.

Part 3

Developing as a Teacher of Teachers

Introduction

The focus in Part 3 is on the development of the ToT, as a person whose experiences, thinking and skills are critical for the central practice of *teaching* teachers. We discuss ways in which ToTs can develop their own skills, as planners, preparers and also as implementers of the plans they have prepared, in real classrooms with real participants. We see this stage of classroom implementation as the penultimate stage of a process which moves from designing, planning, and preparing to teaching and finally assessing and evaluating, which we look at in Part 4.

From what we have said you might expect Part 3 to focus on ToTs' actual teaching behaviours; indirectly, and to a certain extent, it does this in Chapter 9. However, any ToT's in-class behaviours are affected by a unique combination of factors (actual learners' needs, the nature of a programme and its design, actual plans, available facilities, ToT thinking at the time, prevailing approaches to teaching and ToTing, and the contextually accepted vision of the ultimate goal of teacher learning, to name just a few) which we are unable to predict in detail. This is one reason why Part 3 deals with aspects of ToT development for planning and preparing (which will influence teaching indirectly), and only with some specific aspects of teaching itself.

There are two further reasons for the focus on ToT development here. The first is practical. We expect many readers will be new to teaching teachers, and so personal development is likely to be a particular concern, since as suggested in Part 1 teaching and teaching teachers are two distinct professions. The second is more ideological. We believe that, if ToTs are going to be managing other peoples' professional learning, they need to be capable managers of their own. This is particularly so because, in an investigation–articulation approach to teaching teachers, a ToT's main role is mostly that of manager of learning (and group) processes, and only sometimes that of a 'knower' who 'tells'.

So why is it important for ToTs to be effective managers of their own learning? First of all, the better we all become at managing our own learning, the better we will become at many of the preparatory practices discussed in Part 2, and at managing that of our learners when teaching. We have found that creating opportunities (different types of starting-point experiences for ourselves) for our own development has helped us to better understand what opportunities our learners need and how we might provide them. They after all are also teachers, although a ToT's 'subject' is Teaching while their learners' may be Maths or History, for example.

In addition, we have found ourselves teaching on TL programmes with aims (as some of the ultimate goals we discuss in Chapter 1 require) that included the need for participants to 'learn how to learn' and acquire the capacity to engage in 'lifelong learning', that is be proactive managers of their own learning. In these cases, we needed to try to model our own learning process explicitly in order to provide the learners with observation experiences to support their learning of these skills. We realized that in order to be able to model how we manage our own learning, we needed to be actively engaged in such learning throughout our teaching. This required us to be clear about how to create and take advantage of opportunities for such learning. Over time, we also realized that simple engagement in our own learning was still not enough, since if we wanted it to be 'observable', we also needed to make at least some of it 'visible' to our participants.

Part 3 then deals with the kinds of 'learning opportunities' we have found useful in helping ourselves develop as ToTs, as well as the ways in which we try to make the management of our own learning visible as we teach.

The focus here is on YOUR development as ToTs. However, because you and your course participants are both learning 'teaching' (albeit you of teaching and they of a particular school subject), many of the ideas suggested in Chapter 8 can with slight modification also be profitably used with learners, particularly on in-service programmes.

Chapter 8

ToTs together

We feel strongly that working with other ToTs is one of the most important means of helping ourselves develop the skills we need as individual ToTs. In this chapter we outline some of the many ways in which we believe that working as 'ToTs together' can be helpful. After a discussion of group dynamics, and how an understanding of this has helped us work with and in groups, we look at a range of development opportunities that may be provided by working as ToTs together in such groups. We emphasize opportunities that support learning for the practices of planning and preparation.

8.1 ToT Development groups

ToT meetings in groups can provide valuable opportunities for development. However, for this time to be as productive as possible (and of benefit to all), this gathering of ToTs needs to become a 'group' in more than just name. So, before discussing how a ToT group can be used, we will first look at what we mean by creating a 'group', and how this might affect what happens in TOTs' meetings.

8.1.1 On group dynamics

We expect like us you will have had experience of working with some classes that have felt like a single unit and others that have felt like a number of separate individuals. You may also have noticed that teaching the class of individuals seemed less enjoyable and/or successful. Through managing our own learning, starting from our experience of working with classes of both types, we became aware of the difference that each type made to the classroom atmosphere as well as the learning outcomes, and so began to look for helpful information about groups through turning to the literature on group dynamics.

We will begin by listing some of the most important things we discovered about groups and then go on to say in what ways they made a difference to what we now do, before discussing their relevance to your 'ToTs together' group.

Groups go through predictable phases of 'group life'. Each phase is equally important and requires certain conditions to be met before the subsequent phase can take place. The phases can be seen simply as a beginning phase, a middle phase and an ending phase, and there are different challenges for both the group leader and its members at each phase.

Successfully managing *the beginning phase* involves the group paying attention to three things:

- ensuring that everybody knows everybody else and develops trusting relationships
- creating agreement about ways of working together and any 'rules' for group membership
- agreeing shared group goals

At *the middle phase* the emphasis turns to:

- maintaining the group focus
- resolving any conflicts that may arise between members
- re-negotiating shared group goals as appropriate
- continuing to pay attention to strengthening the, by now, trusting relationships between members

The ending phase is different again, with three main requirements:

- reviewing the shared experience
- reviewing the learning or other achievements of the group
- ensuring that individual members have what they need to continue their learning without the support of the group

How has all this made a difference to our practice of teaching or working with any group? One way is that it has affected how we approach the planning phases of courses. We now allocate a lot more time than we used to at the beginning and end for the important group formation and disbanding stages.

The beginning phase

From the first moment of coming together, whether at the first 'ToTs together' meeting or at the first session on a programme such as that illustrated in Part 2, we pay explicit attention to helping the group form as quickly as possible, and may spend a whole morning, or longer, mainly on this. In some groups people know each other (by name at least) and in others they do not. Even where members of some groups know each other, it is unlikely that everyone knows everybody and we almost certainly will not know everyone's names. Our first task is therefore always to provide opportunities for members/participants to find out each others' names and a little personal information. In early sessions, or meetings, we emphasize re-pairing and re-grouping activities to allow members to get to know each other, and pay particular attention ourselves to memorizing and using each member's/participant's name as well as any personal information about them as we learn it.

Even on formally designed courses, where we may already have heard individually what participants' wants are as part of the needs analysis process, we revisit these during the beginning phase so that everyone has a real chance to participate in the agreement of shared goals. To the extent that individuals are clear about their personal reasons for being in the group or on the course and are willing to divulge them at such an early stage of group life, this agreement of shared goals can help prevent misunderstandings and conflict later on.

Finally, we explicitly discuss what expectations we have of each other in terms of participation, tasks, timings, breaks and, if these 'rules' get 'broken', we renegotiate them. For example, if on Day 1 of a course it is agreed that the morning coffee break will be 15 minutes, but in fact we find that after a few days participants are never on time to resume work, we discuss this. If we then find that it takes most of the break actually to obtain the coffee, the group may agree to make the break 30 minutes and to adjust the timing of the lunchtime break.

The findings of research on group dynamics have been an extremely useful conceptual tool for us and one that we now consciously consider in our planning of programmes and sessions, as well as at the start of new ToTs together groups. This has led us to collect a range of strategies, activities, games and techniques that we can use in the management of group processes. Our draft programme and first session plans in Chapters 5 and 6 give examples of how we try to take group dynamics into consideration and of activities we often use to begin the group-forming process.

Although we are specifically talking about group dynamics here within the context of developing ToT learning, we hope that you can see that it is also critical to enabling teacher learning. First, having a real group helps create the safe atmosphere that is one of the necessary conditions for people to be willing to articulate their thinking and try out different practices. Also it is the contributions of group members (which will only be made if they feel safe and have time within the programme to make them) that allow the whole group to gain different perspectives on issues under discussion and so develop a richer, more varied or more complete understanding.

The middle phase

With respect to this middle phase, we discovered that in some ways of describing the stages of group life it is thought that a group typically goes through a 'storming' phase (Tuckman 1965*) of disagreement. Knowing that this is a stage that often has to happen before groups can work effectively together has given us the confidence (when members of groups that we have been part of or working with have strongly disagreed or 'stormed') not to panic when it happens. It has also motivated us to look further for ideas about how to manage and resolve 'interpersonal conflict' of this kind.

We try to remember that this 'storming' phase shows that the group has moved on to begin the middle phase of group life in which people no longer feel that they have to be polite (as with strangers) but feel comfortable enough to reveal their real views. This stage may be triggered by disagreements over ideas or behaviour arising from genuine professional belief differences or from individuals having different personal goals for group membership (for example 'mostly to learn' versus 'mostly to socialize' versus 'mostly for local "political" reasons'). Whatever the reason, people's honest views are essential if everyone is to be able to learn more about the 'whole elephant' of whatever is creating 'the storm'. We have found it helps at this stage if we remind ourselves and our colleagues to avoid getting 'personal' (it is not the person, but the idea or behaviour that is controversial), that everyone has reasons for thinking or behaving as they do and that it would be helpful/interesting to try and find out what experiences have brought people to such beliefs or ways of behaving.

We see the key to resolving disagreements at the 'storming' phase as communication within a basically trusting, non-judgemental relationship, and have tried to train ourselves to think about the possible causes and make group time to explore what lies behind the external conflict. When we have managed 'the storm' successfully, we have found that groups can and do come to appreciate rather than feel threatened by different points of view and the group settles down. This is the start of the period of group life when the most productive work can occur and since it is in all group members' interests to reach this point as soon as possible, we believe in putting real effort into creating the group.

Another challenge in the middle phase can be one of group 'maintenance'. All groups can get a bit set in their ways, with the same people sitting in the same places and talking to the same colleagues week after week. Continuing to pay attention to providing opportunities for everyone to maintain their relationships with everyone else by, for example, using re-grouping and re-pairing activities on a regular basis is therefore also important. A further aspect of group maintenance is to revisit periodically the shared group goals. We have often begun a learning process by thinking that we need to learn one thing, only to discover as we began how complex it really is, that we have been over-ambitious, and that there are in fact more stages involved in achieving the goal than we originally realized. On other occasions we have thought we wanted to learn one thing, but an intervening experience (in our ToTing) makes it more urgent or relevant to learn something else entirely. Both of these show that it is important from time to time to confirm agreement that we still wish to follow our original group goals or, if we do not, to adjust them as necessary.

The ending phase

Some groups have a clear end. Others are not time-bound and here the challenge is to recognize when the group has achieved its shared goals and no longer needs to exist in its current form. Sometimes signs that might be taken to show that the group has reached the end of its 'natural life', such as members not coming to meetings, may in fact be indications of an unresolved storming phase (see above) or of the group never really having been formed in the first place.

At this ending phase, if the group has been effective and cohesive, members will feel sad that it is ending. Time therefore needs to be allowed for members to say their personal goodbyes, noting that the next stage of the relationship will be different now they are not meeting regularly.

In terms of the support that the group gave to members' learning, consideration needs to be given to whether the establishment of some form of ongoing, informal, perhaps more virtual, mutual aid group may be appropriate. If it is decided that this would be desirable, then time needs to be provided to agree its role and to exchange the necessary postal addresses, phone numbers or email details. If members are going to continue their learning alone without any further group support, it is important to try and make sure that everyone has been equipped with the conceptual tools and/or resources to do so before this final phase is reached.

Finally, group and group-supported individual achievement and learning needs to be made explicit and celebrated. This is not just so that members can pat each other on the back, but also because any learner needs to leave a learning group with a sense of achievement if they are to approach their next learning endeavour positively. For more detailed ideas of the kinds of activities that could be used at this phase see Malderez and Bodoczky (1999: 148–50).

Even though a 'ToT together' group is a meeting of peers, the group process needs explicit attention. All groups need to agree either that one person will act as leader to bear the above issues in mind and manage stages of the group process, or that the role will be shared among the group, or rotated.

If the group is a voluntary coming together of ToTs you might be tempted to skip or rush the group-forming phase, perhaps because you know each other quite well as people and have all chosen to attend. However, we feel this is unwise. People will rarely know everyone quite as well as they think, and it is still important to establish goals and 'rules' for ways of working. Where 'ToT together' groups are 'compulsory' with members required to attend by 'higher authorities', a leader is likely to be already designated. Since people are less likely to know each other, and have not necessarily chosen to be group members, it will be even more important to manage group processes sensitively. Ideally, any 'designated leader' of a peer ToTs together group would see this management of the group process as their prime concern.

All teachers are 'designated leaders' in their classrooms by virtue of the power of their role. Very few of them, in our experience, take their role of group leader into account in their thinking. ToTs can help them both to become aware of the necessity to manage group processes and be able to do so, by modelling effective management of group processes during the programme, and making explicit what they are doing and why. Learning how to lead and manage group processes through doing it in a ToTs together group is one way of developing such skills.

8.2 Some activities for ToTs together groups

We turn now to some ideas for what you can do together in your formed ToT group and how this might support your development.

8.2.1 Sharing experiences of 'receiving training'

One important role of ToT group meetings (especially for new ToTs) is the opportunity they can offer to get at our own intuitive beliefs about what being a ToT means and looks like in terms of the relationship between ToT and participants. Just as learners will have an internal model of what being a teacher involves, stemming from their long years of experience in schools, so ToTs will have preconceptions born from their experience as learner teachers, of being on the 'receiving end' of ToT activity. Contexts of teaching teachers include not only the 'place', or a consideration of 'where' it occurs, but also of time or 'when' it occurred and 'who' was involved. Features of all of these will have changed since even your most recent memories of 'receiving ToTing'. Talking about the kinds of models of ToTing to which members have been exposed can help in identifying why people hold the views that they do about 'what it means to be a ToT', as well as what those views are.

Even where systems for teaching teachers have remained stable since you were learner-teachers, what is known about teacher learning and how to support it is increasing all the time and will be having more or less impact on current ToT practice. A conscious appreciation of differences in context and of developing understandings of teacher learning has helped us, the writers, to re-examine our intuitive, taken-for-granted beliefs about, for example, the need for ToTs to:

- know (or seem to know) everything
- cover 'everything' in the plan
- stand on the podium and lecture
- dress in a certain way (smarter than or in the same manner as the participants)

Discussion of ToTs' experiences of their prior 'training' can therefore also help group members reconsider some of their beliefs about what a ToT ought to know and/or how a ToT should behave, as well as help the group understand that no one style of ToT behaviour is likely to be totally appropriate or suit everyone.

One technique for managing the above activity (devised by a colleague in Hungary, who got the idea from Personal Construct Theory (Kelly 1970) is as follows:

- Each group member writes down the names of three people who taught them to become (or develop as) a teacher on 3 small bits of paper.
- You take two of the three bits of paper at random.
- Looking at the two names, you ask yourself the question, *what are the similarities between the two and how are they different from the name on the other piece of paper?* (e.g. Ms A and Mr B were fun, but Mr C was dull).
- You write down the two descriptive terms (here, e.g., 'fun' and 'dull') you have given for the differences and similarities.
- Repeat this step an infinite number of times, each time adding another two descriptive terms to your two lists of words. You will probably find that you put what you consider to be more positive descriptions in one list and more negative in the other.
- Keep doing the same thing until you just can't think of any more ways of describing similarities and differences. This gets harder but it is important to keep trying since the ultimate point is to 'unearth' things you may not have been conscious of before (some of the content of your 'undermind'). One way of helping yourself to keep trying is to do the whole process in pairs and for your partner to insist that you answer the question *'how were these two the same but different from this one?'*
- You end up with two longish lists. The idea is that these lists are likely to represent some aspects of the positive and negative models that underpin your ToTing behaviour.
- One way to question these models is then to compare and contrast your lists with somebody else's. You may, for example, notice that, whereas you put 'strict' in your negative list, others have it on the positive side. You may find if you discuss this, that you are actually describing different behaviour, or that the same kind of behaviour (probably from different people) was unhelpful for you but helpful for your colleague.

These lists, and the discussions that follow from them, can help you realize (and so make conscious, and so be in a position to change) some of the preconceptions that you bring to your work as ToTs.

The same types of discussion can be initiated after a starting point 'recalling of past experience' activity such as a drawing of a typical scene from the 'training room' you were a learner teacher in, or a visualization activity (see Malderez and Bodoczky 1999: ch.3, 45–6, for how to conduct a visualization).

8.2.2 Stories

Traditional stories

All cultures have a stock of ancient stories which have long had an essentially teaching purpose. The 'blind men and the elephant' story we told in Chapter 1 is an example. Some authors (e.g. Owen 2001 – see Further reading, p. 139) have collected together stories of this type that can be used in ToT situations to provide a starting-point experience of a metaphorical/affective nature. So one potentially fruitful activity ToTs can engage in together is the collecting and sharing of such stories which, as well as supporting their own learning, are likely to be meaningful to the learners with whom they will be working in their context. This is not to say that we only use stories from the culture of our course participants, but if access to other resources is limited, these local stories that can be used to connect to a variety of themes are readily available in almost any culture, and can be particularly useful in getting people to think about their own attitudes and possible alternatives.

Personal stories

The sharing of stories (in this case 'of teaching teachers') is a common way of bonding, though slightly gendered in certain cultures. In our own culture, we have found that women seem to enjoy this more and find this easier to do than men. Depending on where you are, if there are a lot of men in your group you may have to wait a while before beginning this form of sharing!

There are some writers (Elbaz 1991 – see Further reading, p. 139) who believe that teacher knowledge is itself 'storied', by which they mean that we draw on a set of cases or scenarios in our heads, to enable us to react quickly (with our intuitive KT skills) to the multiple unpredictable events of the classroom. Sharing stories of particular ToT classroom experiences as in the procedure set out below benefits both the storyteller and the listeners.

For the storyteller, the story becomes the description of a starting-point experience from which personal transformative learning can occur. The main benefit for listeners from exposure to what Ur (1996 – see References, p. 138) calls 'vicarious experience', comes through a process of contrasting the story they are listening to with their own sets of stories and the self-questioning that can result. It may also be reassuring and/or enlightening to hear what others are concerned with, take for granted or worry about. So, story-sharing may, for the storyteller, raise awareness of ways of dealing with similar future situations, and for the listeners raise awareness of the range of issues that may arise as a ToT and/or provide reassurance that they are not the only ones having such experiences. For groups in early stages of development the first stories could of course be those relating to a perceived 'success' and so less potentially threatening. (We have found that in telling our success stories, by the time we had gone through the process below, they did not always seem as totally successful as we originally thought they had been! However, the process helped us, not only to consider what elements contributed to 'success', but also to uncover some new ideas about how to be even more successful next time).

Our teaching teachers stories

General instructions

- Work in groups of three.
- Take turns to tell a 'something intriguing' or a 'sticky moment' story from your own experience as Step 1 and follow the five steps below carefully.

- Aim for about 15 minutes per 'turn' (all 5 steps). Note that 'turn 1' may take a little longer than the subsequent ones, because Step 3, in particular, will become easier/quicker for the group.

When it is NOT your turn

- Listen well! In particular:
- WAIT until the person whose turn it is has finished talking (Steps 1 and 4) or invites your ideas (Steps 2, 3, 5)
- Be ready to ask clarification questions (Steps 1 and 4), or provide any additional ideas you have (Steps 2, 3, 5).

When it IS your turn

Step 1: Tell your story

- Include information on: who, where, when, what happened, what you thought/felt/did, what 'they' did/seemed to think/feel, what happened then.
- Check other group members have a clear picture of the situation – add any other details if asked.

Step 2: 'Think aloud' about as many possible meanings/explanations as you can

- Start with what you thought at the time – brainstorm as many new/ different possible explanations as you can. (Don't censor any ideas at this stage, however unlikely or 'wild' they might seem!)
- Invite other group members to add any other possible explanations they can think of.

Step 3: Recall as many 'conceptual tools' – theories about learning to be a teacher, or teaching teachers – as you can

(See Chapter 1 and ideas from Further reading pp. 138–40).

- List/briefly describe all the theories you have learnt/read about which might be relevant to deciding which of your explanations at Step 2 is most likely.
- Invite group members to describe briefly any other theories they know which might be relevant.

Step 4: 'Think aloud' about outcomes from Steps 2 and 3

- Compare explanations from Step 2 and theories from Step 3 and decide how you would now explain the situation in your story.
- Check if group members follow the logic in your decision-making process. (Are you using other information you did not provide in Step 1?)

Step 5: So what? 'Think aloud' about what you could/will do differently next time

- Based on your chosen explanation(s), brainstorm what you could do (say/think/notice) differently 'next time'.
- Invite other group members to add any other possible ideas.
- Decide what you WILL do. Imagine yourself doing it in practice and describe what you see to group members.

When everyone has had a turn

Consider *what* you have learnt, and *how*. What do you want/need to learn next?

8.2.3 Reading groups

Some reading groups we have belonged to have an underlying theory–application approach in that they begin by doing some reading, and then follow this with discussions on how ideas might be 'applied', without any prior connection to individual experience. We have talked above about the importance of stories (sometimes called cases) and of sharing these for practitioner knowledge development. One way of ensuring that members of a reading group don't feel that they are participating in a purely theory–application group that is disconnected from their own experience is to adopt a storied approach to the selection of things to be read. Each member of the group selects a reading that has genuinely helped them to explain an aspect of experience, to plan how to give participants particular kinds of learning opportunities or has influenced their attitudes towards their work in some important (to them) way.

The person selecting the reading is therefore telling a personal story of their own development in which the conceptual tools derived from the reading were a useful piece of Step 3 input into one of their own self-managed learning sequences, or the practical ideas contained within the reading helped them to make decisions at Step 5 (see the five steps, Chapter 3). The first session of a reading group might deal principally with process needs (see 8.1.1 on group dynamics above) before the first selector tells their story of how they found the reading useful. This acts as a motivator to the other readers, to recall similar or different experiences of their own to bring to their own reading of the text. Members read the text before the next session, which then consists of general group discussion about the content and utility of the reading. Where genuine differences of opinion emerge this may highlight differences in participants' beliefs and/or in the contexts in which they work. This recognition of contextual differences can potentially encourage all group members to ask themselves questions such as the following when they read:

- Who are the authors and who are they writing for?
- What context (time, place) do they come from?
- How are their ideas and context similar to or different from my own?

Any reading group session then ends with the next selector telling the story connected with the reading they have chosen.

8.2.4 Sharing tasks, activities, games and techniques

All practitioners are magpies! (A magpie is a bird that in Britain is known as being attracted by shiny things and has, for example, been known to steal a ring from a kitchen windowsill. So anyone who likes collecting attractive things from different places, we call, metaphorically, a 'magpie'.) As ToTs we consider our-selves as magpies, in the sense that we like to collect different things for learners to do in our classrooms to add to our teaching 'kitbag' or 'toolkit', and feel that the more options we have, the more precisely we will be able to tailor the learning opportunities that we offer our participants to their particular needs.

So one further thing you might do in your 'ToTs together' group is to take turns demonstrating (and letting other ToTs experience) a particular technique, game, activity or task that you use, which you believe other ToTs might not know or do not use. The demonstration might usefully be followed by discussion on how, when, why and whether members might use it, whether other members wish to add it to the contents of their kitbags, as well as whether such members feel they need practice opportunities before using it themselves. Similarly, the ToT group meeting can provide a safe environment for practising anything you have all just learned about, and so help develop both your ToT teaching skills and your confidence in your ability to use the new idea. ToT group meetings are also a useful venue for trying out any newly created game, activity or task before using it with participants. Here the trying out enables the creator to see how colleagues react and to get their comments or thoughts to inform revisions before its actual use. The trying-out process thus potentially helps in both the 'materials design' itself, and the development of materials design skills.

8.2.5 Sharing handouts

On the theme of materials design, one or more ToT group meetings could be spent comparing and discussing handouts, perhaps those used to support the teaching of an agreed theme or topic. The discussion could cover issues to do with handout formats (see Chapter 6. 1.3), or task and activity design (e.g. do they seem likely to 'do' what you hope they will, are they fit-for-purpose? are the instructions clear?), as well as how colleagues (and their participants) actually use the handouts. Again this provides a chance for ToT members to act as 'magpies', but also to rethink the underlying messages that various forms of handouts might be sending to parti-cipants.

8.2.6 Writing group

The central activity supported or done here is writing. One form is 'Journaling groups' where ToTs come to meetings with their ToT journals, or spend the first part of meetings writing an individual journal entry for sharing with other members of the group. Part of the meeting might be spent discussing similarities or differences between the concerns revealed by the journal entries. Alternatively the group might agree to allow some time during the meeting for individual members to support each other in reviewing a number of their journal entries to identify 'progress' and/or any issue that they would like to turn into a personal learning goal.

Another form of writing group might be one in which individual members bring drafts of some professional writing to the group, for an insider-reader perspective and comment. If the writing is for other ToTs the writing group provides a safe forum to try out the effectiveness of the writing for the target readership.

Writing groups can also consist of larger, more formal or collaborative writing projects, based round the production of an article for a professional journal or the creation of an edited publishable volume. As well as contributing towards the achievement of the ultimate goal of professionalism, writing groups can provide further genuine reasons to dialogue and explore and understand each other's perspectives. Where ToTs are also members of Higher Education institutions, a writing group may find ways to combine their professional interests with research requirements, and support to develop their writing into more academically acceptable forms. This work could be based on extensive desk research, or on action or some other form of practitioner research. (Our small 'writing group of 2' has certainly helped us to both clarify and articulate thoughts and experiences!)

Chapter 9

Working together to develop in-class teaching skills

The kind of learning that a ToT might have derived from the suggested activities for ToTs together groups in Chapter 8 can directly affect the preparatory practices of designing, planning and preparation. Indirectly, of course, changes to these will affect actual teaching too. In this chapter we see the suggestions we make for ToT development as more directly influencing what a ToT says and does as an in-class manager of others' professional learning. This, of course, will in turn indirectly affect preparatory practices.

What follows then are some suggestions for how ToTs can work together both in the classroom and outside in ToTs together groups, to develop the in-class aspect of their work.

9.1 Team teaching

We suggest that, if it is at all possible when working on a course with groups of participants, it is useful to 'team-teach' with another ToT. By this we do not mean simply (or even) dividing up the work to be done on a course and each taking particular sessions, although if the designing and planning stages of course development are shared, this would of course provide 'thinking' development opportunities. By team-teaching here, we mean both ToTs being present in every session, with both 'prepared' (preparation of self) for the whole session, although decisions may have been made about who will 'front' which part. Team-ToTing on courses for teachers naturally supports both partners' development, through the inevitable talk about and for the course, the exposure to each others' 'performance styles', and the opportunities for comparing and contrasting what was noticed during each session. In addition, it allows partners to 'play to their strengths'. For example one ToT might be particularly good at demonstrating techniques, while the other is skilled at eliciting ('getting out'). Everybody benefits here. Participants get the 'best' session possible, ToTs can feel confident in what they are doing, while also observing how their partner copes with an aspect of the work they feel less comfortable with. Over time, as everyone (ToTs and participants) feels more comfortable with each other, ToT A may feel able to try out a part of a session that ToT B has modelled in earlier sessions, and so expand their own range of skills.

9.2 Peer observation

Peer observation represents another form of sharing that may of course be integrated into team-teaching. There is nothing more useful for you, when you are trying to improve a particular aspect of your work, than to invite another pair of eyes in (or into) the room to 'notice' one or more aspects of what is going on. You might ask your observer, for example, to focus on the words that you actually use when giving instructions for a task, or how the way you work seems to affect a particular participant or group of participants. As a ToT, from the middle of teaching so to speak, it is difficult to keep a 'helicopter view' of all that is going on in the classroom. This is especially true if you are particularly concerned with one or more aspects of your own behaviour, as all ToTs inevitably are in the early stages of their careers as ToTs, as well as in the first sessions with a new group of participants. If you can add what someone else has noticed to your own observations it will be easier, after the lesson, to consider whether your work has had the effects you planned, and what, if anything, you might try differently another time.

Your peer observer's role during the session is to try to notice anything you have requested, and then in subsequent discussions, to act, in effect, as a mentor working with an experienced and skilled mentee – you (see Chapter 7). It will be particularly important that, when you are an observer, you try not to reveal the judgements you will almost inevitably have made about any colleagues' teaching. There are four reasons for this. The first is that you can destroy a trusting relationship a lot more easily than you can build one, and judgements may be perceived as hurtful. The second is that even if your judgement is not hurtful, it is nonetheless an outsider's viewpoint and not necessarily helpful. What matters here is what the observed ToT him/herself concludes from the experience and what action they take as a result. Thirdly, your judgement may be wrong because you may lack much relevant information. It is unlikely that you will know exactly what was in the teacher's mind, or what the history of the relationships between teacher and participants has been. Your interpretation of what you have noticed may also be based on the result of your missing something the teacher did notice but you did not. A final reason for avoiding rushing to make judgements is that often neither ToT may be in a position to decide whether a teaching session has been effective, in the sense of 'adding to' learners' necessary knowledge, until some later opportunity to see its impact on learners' actual teaching is available, (see Part 4).

9.3 Teaching skill development in ToTs together groups

One option for ToT groups is to focus their work on the teaching phase of the ToT practices' sequence. In order to make this relevant to the particular group members, it may be useful to carry out an individual and a group needs analysis, which will in fact probably be more of a 'wants analysis'. On the basis of the outcome of this, the group can first of all decide whether there is any match between individual group members' 'wants' for development of aspects of in-class teaching and other group members' knowledge of these aspects. Where there is, and where a majority of group members' wants coincide, and a minority of members feel that they do have the desired knowledge, a group session can be arranged in which the knowledgeable member(s) lead. Similar one-to-one arrangements outside group time may also be possible. Where knowledge does not exist within the group and where the 'want' seems to be important to everyone, the group may be able to find a visiting ToT to help them.

For the remainder of this chapter we are imagining that you (readers) and we (authors) are an informal group of ToTs. While there are bound to be many contextual needs that you could help us learn about, we suppose that for many of you it might be difficult to work out how to manage certain aspects of the actual teaching in an investigation–articulation approach, since it is so different from the theory–application approach that most of us have experienced. To be successful using the latter approach ToTs had to know the content and then 'deliver' it, often in very formal lectures. Most of what we have discussed so far in this book, however, requires different knowledge and behaviour. There are three issues in particular that new ToTs may find it helpful to explore in such ToT development groups, and, as imaginary 'knowledgeable ToTs' in 'our' group, we discuss them next.

9.3.1 The management of small-group work

It is worth noting here that 'group work' is a form of classroom organization, it is not a task, activity or game in itself, although all of these can be done in groups. Successful group work depends on two things: what people are being asked to do in the groups, and how the ToT manages the group.

What people are being asked to do in the groups

By this we refer again to the need to make instructions for learner tasks focus on what the learners have to do and produce, and to the need to make sure that the purpose for the activity is clearly relevant to the particular participants rather than merely reflecting (possibly more theoretical) ToT aims. For example as a ToT you may want them to discuss a particular topic or experience in order to 'get out' and so get at their current thinking, or to discuss a new input to develop their thinking further. To do either of these by just telling them to *please discuss this* will not necessarily seem meaningful to the learners, nor does it give them information about how to do it or what outcome is expected.

We find group work is much more successful if we give them a specific task. In other words rather than just saying *please discuss this* (which is an instruction but not a task), we pay attention in our spoken or written instructions to specifying both what they are supposed to do and what outcome we expect of the activity. The kind of instructions for group work that we might give at a Step 4 stage (see Chapter 3) might for example be: *Look at the different viewpoints expressed on the handout and agree together which one is the most relevant in your context*, or, *Look at the different viewpoints expressed on the handout and rank these according to their importance to you as a group.* In both of these tasks our aim is to get participants to think, and discuss and compare and contrast, but this should happen naturally as they engage together in accomplishing the outcome of the task (for more on tasks see Willis 1996). When we find that small group work does not seem to work, the first thing we ask ourselves is 'what am I asking them to do? Have I given them clear 'task' instructions?'

How the ToT manages the group work

Even if you have got a clear task for participants to accomplish during the group work, there are several other issues to consider:

- training participants to be effective group members
- group size
- group membership
- group stability (do people always work in the same groups or not?)
- Monitoring group work
- Managing the reporting back process

Training participants to be effective group members

In contexts where a theory–application approach has been common throughout the education system, learners as well as ToTs may find the move to small-group work difficult and so will need support in making it effective. Some ways of introducing group work were suggested by 'the blind man and the elephant' story or the 'line-up in terms of years of expertise' grouping activity, both of which aim to highlight the experience that already exists within the whole group and so the need to share it. Practically speaking group members may need support in how to get the most out of activities conducted in small groups and we have found it useful to include something like the following on the handout before the first group-work task. Please note that these are not the only ways to talk about roles within a group and there are many other suggestions in, e.g., Dornyei and Murphey (2003) – see Further reading, p. 139.

Before the discussion, allocate the following roles:

Task Manager
Job description: Keep the group 'on task', be the time keeper and ensure 'the job is done' within the time limit.

Harmoniser

Job description: Ensure everyone's opinion is 'heard'. Mediate if necessary in case of dispute. Synthesize views.

Reporter

Job description: Keep notes. Check you have the group's agreement on what to report. Be ready to report task outcome (and any relevant information on task process) to the whole group when the task is complete.

After the group work, especially in the early days and more occasionally throughout the course, it is worth spending a little time asking the groups to discuss how well they felt they worked together, how they could become more effective and any feedback to individual group members regarding their impact in the role that they had chosen or been given. We suggest that, to start with, everyone tries out each of the above roles. Having tried them all, people may find that they are naturally better at one type of role than another, and may therefore wish to take on this role more often. Conversely, you may want to encourage them, particularly in situations where the achievement of the task outcome in the allocated time is less critical, to practise those roles that they find less instinctively 'easy'.

Group size

For small-group work it is generally accepted that groups of more than four or five will be ineffective, since if you think of real life, this number is about the maximum possible if everyone is to be able to participate in and maintain a single conversation.

Group membership

A number of issues may make particular groupings of participants more or less problematic. These may be culture or subject-specific or more personal. They may include for example, status or gender issues, subject-related similarities or differences, differing levels of existing knowledge (e.g. in modern foreign languages, levels of language proficiency), or particular friendships and personalities. As a general rule people who get on well together as friends can work effectively together on tasks where there needs to be a product, but if the task requires the sharing of different opinions you may want to mix the groups up more to get a wider variety of opinion expressed.

Group stability

As is clear from what we say above, depending on the nature of the work to be undertaken, having the same people in the same group throughout may not be appropriate. Having said this, if you are working with a very large number of participants you may want to aim for some stability at least to start with in order to try to meet the need for belonging and to create a safe psychological atmosphere.

Monitoring group work

Unlike with pupils in schools the monitoring function for ToTs does not have a strong behaviour management function, although we often still see some 'guilty' faces as we approach groups or individuals who are 'off-task'! Monitoring does involve physically moving around the different groups and the main purpose here is to diagnose difficulties and be helpful (by which we mean scaffolding – see 9.3.2), as well as to gauge how long people are taking and what this implies for the rest of the session and the plan. When working with groups you may want to consider the best way of being physically close to the group; do you stand, squat, kneel or pull up a chair? If you remain standing you can pause for a short time, but it might be intimidating. If you pull up a chair it suggests you will be there for some time and, as you look more like a group member, you may end up doing the task for them. Kneeling or squatting might be better, but this assumes your knees, unlike ours, are still flexible enough!

Managing the reporting back process

We talk first about what managing the reporting back process might mean for ToT attitude and thinking. Two aspects are relevant here, relating to why and how to listen to post-group-work reports as a ToT.

The first thing to say is that all groups deserve to be listened to seriously, partly because they will always have potentially interesting things to say, and partly because there is rarely if ever a totally 'right answer' anyway (even though you may have an ideal one in mind), and therefore even responses that don't fit your hoped-for outcome may be relevant and, more than this, may help all (including you) learn. Provided they can explain why they have come to it, whatever conclusion a group might come to, even if in your judgement it is partial or incomplete, is bound to be legitimate for them, and so interesting to you for the glimpses it gives you of how they see 'the elephant' and what experiences have led them to this view. There may be occasions where you feel that they have not actually been focusing on the 'elephant' (the desired topic or content) at all. This, rather than being automatically worthy of your condemnation, is more likely to suggest that some aspect of your task, or how you have managed it, has not worked (see 9.3.2). So your first main reason for listening is one of 'diagnosis' – of what and how groups think, and possibly also to judge the effectiveness of your task design and management.

Your second purpose for listening connects to your ToT session aims. Depending on what step or stage of the pendulum swing the activity is supposed to support, your purpose for listening will be slightly different. For example, if the group-work activity or task is at the Step 2 stage (sharing explanations of experience), you will need to listen out for links to any input you hope to give later, or to judge whether, after all groups have reported back and you have synthesized the discussion outcomes, your proposed input is needed at all. If you conclude that it isn't, because everything you wanted to say has emerged from the collected task outcomes, you may still need to provide the technical language for what has been discussed, perhaps through your synthesis. If, on the other hand, the group-work is at Step 4 or 5 stage and people have been discussing all the previous stages and what these might imply for the next stage, you will probably want to list the groups' practical ideas, perhaps adding some more, and help learners prepare for the future with questions like: *Which can you see yourself doing? What would it look like? What practical preparations do you need to make to be able to do it? How will it fit in with the book?* etc.

There are of course practical organizational aspects of managing the reporting stage. These include:

- deciding, at the previous planning and preparation phases, on which groups will report in which order
- deciding how they will be reporting (orally, OHTs, posters)
- deciding what the listening groups are asked to do while they listen (e.g. compare what they hear with their own conclusions/outcomes)
- considering whether a hand-in of all task outcomes is being or will be created and who is/will be responsible for this

So, as can be seen, the use and management of small-group work, is a key feature of any approach for supporting teacher learning which attempts to move away from a process which sees learning as being principally about applying theories. A term that we mentioned above in the section on monitoring small-group work is *scaffolding*, and we now turn to consider what this term can mean for ToT practice.

9.3.2 Scaffolding

The whole process of supporting teacher learning suggests – through the word 'support' – being helpful. But 'helpful' here does not usually refer to 'help' in the everyday sense of the word which frequently has a sense of 'doing things for somebody'. For example, when a colleague sees us struggling with too many bags of books as we walk to the car park, and asks *'Can I help you?'* what they usually mean is *'Can I carry some of those for you?'* They offer to carry in our stead – to do it for us. Learning is not usually supported by help of this kind. Another maxim of ours is therefore *'Never do for the learners what they can do for themselves'*, since if we do the thinking or 'doing' (analysing, designing, planning, teaching – whatever activity) *for* our learners, they will never learn to do it for themselves. Not only does this maxim save a ToT time and effort (in one sense, while demanding it in another), but more importantly thinking like this increases the number and type of learning opportunities that we provide (see our definition of 'teacher' in the introduction to this book).

The maxim above reminds us that another enjoyable activity in ToT together groups is to share maxims; members telling them to each other with the story behind them, and describing what effect, if any, they have on what they actually do in practice.

The kind of 'help' that *is* supportive of learning has been called 'scaffolding', a term coined by Wood *et al* (1976) – see Further reading, p. 140 – to talk about the particular kind of support that teachers of all kinds provide for their learners. Before we talk further about scaffolding let's give you an example of scaffolding in action through a transcript of an actual event that happened to one of us. [Notice what the son does to help the mother learn how to use the new VCR – yes, this was some years ago!]

'Scaffolding' in action

Son: So what am I showing you?

Mother: How do I get this thing to work?

S: Press the 'standby' button.

(M presses.)

S: Put the video in.

(M puts video cassette in slot.)

S: Get the video remote.

(M reaches for TV remote.)

S: No, the video remote.

M: (Looking around) Which one's that?

S: You know which one it is! (looking towards coffee table).

(M 'finds' right one on coffee table, and nods, looking from the other, TV remote, to the one in her hand.)

S: Press 'play'.

(M presses button on remote marked 'play', looks at TV – content of video cassette not visible on screen.)

M: See! It's not on!

S: (patient explanatory tone) We're on TV not the video channel. Find the TV-slash-Video button.

(M looks at video remote in her hand and presses button marked TV/VCR – looks at screen where the contents of video cassette are now playing.)

S: Yes, that's it! See? You can do it!

The things that you may have noticed as you read are in fact some of the main features of scaffolding. We notice the following:

The son

- checked they both understood the goal of the exercise
- broke the process down into steps
- let the mother press the buttons, put the cassette in and find the remote herself: he didn't do it for her
- reminded her of what she already knew which would be useful in the present learning situation ('You know which one it is' – she knew which the TV

remote was, and could use this knowledge to 'work out' that the other one in the room must be the video remote)

- didn't give unnecessary information when he could see it wasn't needed (e.g. say exactly where the TV/Video button was)
- encouraged/showed faith in his learner ('you know which one it is! ... See? You can do it!')

The mother

- explained her goal
- carried out the actions
- explained what the problem was when she encountered it ('See! It's not on!')
- and through this dialogue and supported process successfully used the VCR on this occasion.

Even if there is a successful outcome, it usually takes more than one scaffolded attempt at doing something for someone to be able to say they have 'learned' how to do it well enough to do it effectively on their own. If, however, we follow our above maxim ('never do for somebody what they can do for themselves') later attempts should need less and less 'help' or scaffolding. In order to judge what help is still needed the scaffolder will have to be patient enough to wait and see how much the learner can now do without support, before intervening with a clue, some information or any of the scaffolding actions such as those above. (In the above example on later occasions without the presence of the son, the mother initially tried alone, but in fact had to resort to some self-administered scaffolding – consulting the transcript – to remind herself of how to get the TV on the video channel!)

There were other important contextual factors that played a role in the event illustrated by the transcript, and that may be relevant to decision-making in any scaffolding situation. These are the physical context, the interpersonal context and the context of dialogue.

The physical context in which the scaffolding takes place may affect what can be learnt, as well as its transferability. In the example above, the event took place in the living-room where all the paraphernalia of British life, then (as now) including a number of remote controls, surrounded the 'teacher' and 'learner'. The learner was in the real-life, messy, imperfect context in which she would need to do the thing she was learning to do. In addition, it took the learner several ever more successful attempts at VCR-using in the context in which she had first needed it and learnt it, before she was able, again at first with 'help', to use 'foreign' VCRs in other contexts. Far too often we expect people to learn teaching away from real classrooms and the real pupils who make the context of teaching complicated and 'messy'. Scaffolding works best when you are scaffolding the action in the context in which it will have to take place. Away from classrooms we can scaffold thinking, or noticing skills development, planning or analysing, and even, through micro-teaching, particular 'performance skills', but the integrated knowledges of actual teaching can only be scaffolded in the real context. This is one important argument for one-to-one school-based mentoring or ToTing.

The degree of understanding, or the interpersonal context, between the scaffolder and the person being scaffolded is also important. In our example above, the son was the teacher of the mother and they both knew each other very well. Of relevance to the particular learning that was being scaffolded is the fact that the son knew the mother was a bit of a technophobe and liable to panic unnecessarily when confronted with technology. The transcript suggests that he took this into account because of his (somewhat uncharacteristic) patience and encouragement. This highlights the great importance of another one of our maxims: you cannot put down stepping stones for someone without knowing where they are. (Claxton 1990). Knowing 'where they are' means not only knowing about what they know but also how they are thinking and feeling and how they are approaching the learning process, in order also to be able to be supportive in an interpersonal or affective sense.

Finally, our example highlights the need for communication, and the role of dialogue in scaffolding encounters. We believe that dialogue is central to all teaching and learning encounters, although it is perhaps particularly noticeable in one-to-one encounters. In the example above, we can see that information was going both ways. The mother through her *'See! It's not on!'* comment was giving information to the son about the precise location of her difficulty. This then enabled him to diagnose that she lacked a specific piece of relevant information (the need to press the VCR TV button) and to provide this. A lot has been written about how central dialogue is to educational processes (from Vygotsky 1962, to Freire 1970, to Bohm 1996) and one way of looking at the approach to teaching teachers suggested in this book is from this dialogic, two-way information flow, perspective. For example, the needs analysis process, the 'getting out before you put in' steps, the procedures for group formation, all require information *from* the learners, before decisions can be made about what 'help' the learners need.

So how can all this help us as ToTs while monitoring small-group work?

We imagine the following scenario as an illustration: as a Step 4 task learners in small groups are asked to rank a number of perspectives on a particular topic according to their usefulness/relevance to them as group.

During early monitoring you notice a participant and/or group sitting doing little, apparently at a loss. It may be appropriate to use the first 'scaffolding move' listed above and check they have 'understood the goal of the exercise'.

However clear we think our task instructions have been, however carefully we have followed our plan to repeat them, as well as check understanding by asking someone to tell us what they are going to do, there has almost always been someone in the group whose attention at that moment had wandered, or who didn't hear/listen. The use of this first scaffolding move as part of the early monitoring, is therefore almost always needed.

Similarly we may discover that an individual, or usually a group, may be clear about the overall task, but not know how to begin it, and scaffolding that helps them to 'break the process down into steps' by asking them, for example, 'So what's the first thing to do? And then?' may be needed.

Just as the son let the mother press the buttons and put the cassette in, etc., if a group is having difficulties ranking ideas, it would not be scaffolding for the ToT to 'give' them their 'answer'. Rather in this case it might be useful to 'remind them of what they already know', or things they have stated (and perhaps discussed earlier in a Step 2 task) and ask them to use this in making a decision. It might also be important to 'show your faith in them' and encourage them to have faith in themselves, perhaps by reminding them of their years of experience, as well as eventually accepting and valuing their conclusions (see reporting back above).

A lot of complicated things have been written about 'scaffolding', but we believe that the simple basic principles, as outlined above, are well worth remembering and trying to use and could be a cornerstone for the effective teaching of a variety of different learners learning different things in different places.

9.3.3 Listening

A third topic that it might be useful for us to work on in our imaginary ToTs together group is listening. It is easy to notice that teachers talk, but you cannot see somebody listening, although you might infer that they are doing so through their body language and subsequent behaviour. Good listening is vital for a ToT because without it they are less effective partners in dialogue, and also because it is a crucial part of their ability to notice (see Chapter 12) and so to scaffold appropriately.

Two clear examples of why a ToT's ability to listen matters have been given in the last two sections. First, if we think back to managing the products of group work, we can see the central role of listening-to-notice in the management of the process. Secondly, if we think about scaffolding, we can see that for a dialogue to be able to be supportive in a 'scaffolding' way, you have first to listen carefully (and perhaps observe) before considering what to say, what support to give next.

Through the type of listening we suggest with groups when 'managing the reporting back process' (see 9.3.1), we try to support as many of our participants as possible. This cannot strictly speaking be scaffolding for every participant, as scaffolding, being an accurate and individualized provision of support, is essentially a one-to-one process. However, when working with an individual teacher in a mentoring process, for example, we do have the chance to be more 'accurate' in our scaffolding. This crucially depends on attentive interpersonal listening, as the mother–son example above demonstrated.

Whether working with groups or individual teachers, we see two main purposes for listening. The first is to listen for the content of their thinking and the second is to listen to the person and how they are feeling.

Reasons for listening to the content of what a teacher says

We have given some purposes for listening in the 'Management of small-group work' section above (9.3.1), which may also be relevant on other occasions. You will be listening to notice not just the existing concepts that participants hold about a topic, but also to try to gauge the extent to which they have taken into consideration, and maybe integrated, what others (including yourself) have said. You are also listening to the content of what they say in terms of the types of topics they talk about so as to gauge their current concerns. This is a form of ongoing needs analysis that may affect your future decisions about the process and sequence of the next stages of the programme.

Reasons for 'listening' to the person and their feelings.

Despite opportunities for discussions and multiple 'inputs', participants may not have been able to take account of others' ideas for a number of personal reasons. Careful interpersonal listening may help the ToT to understand these reasons, which in turn may suggest an appropriate strategy to adopt. We list and discuss a number of the personal reasons, which seemed to stand in the way of learning, that we have encountered.

Level of commitment to their present ways of thinking

If listening to the way a participant speaks suggests a strong commitment to a particular view (often accompanied by a reluctance to consider any others), the ToT may need to work really hard on providing 'starting-point experiences' that will help participants to discover that there are other rational ways of thinking worth considering.

Lack of previous experience of (and so skills in) adjusting their ways of thinking

Sometimes in listening to what someone says or in noticing the difficulties they have in saying it, you become aware that this is something that they have more or less taken for granted hitherto, and have never reconsidered. If this occurs often for a particular participant, it suggests that they are not used to 'reflecting' on their experience, or 'changing their minds'. One strategy we have used to encourage and support new 'professional thinkers', is to model, as a first step in a skill-learning cycle, our own experience of changing our previous ways of thinking, through stories and talking about it explicitly. (I used to think ... but then this happened ... so now I think ...). Another is to be careful in monitoring the discussions in which the participant is engaged and to be ready to scaffold as necessary.

Knowing participants as individuals might also lead us to a conclusion that someone's seeming reluctance to 'change their minds' might be in part because they do not want to be seen to be doing so by other participants. This may happen in contexts where people in authority are expected already to 'know' as well as perhaps maintain a particular publicly accepted point of view. A public 'change of mind' in such circumstances for a 'higher-ranking' course participant may therefore be perceived as undermining their authority. Explicit work on group processes, together with perhaps a group-established confidentiality 'rule', can enable such participants to feel safe enough, and in a sufficiently different environment, to reveal the doubts that inevitably precede changes of mind.

Difficulties in Interpersonal relationships with the 'inputter'

We all have experience of not listening to people we don't like or are annoyed with. As a ToT if you suspect that interpersonal difficulties are causing some participants not to hear you or others, then you need to take time to talk things through using ideas from conflict resolution and/or group dynamics (see Further reading, pp. 138–40).

Invisible contextual issues relating to deeply held, societally determined, values about human beings/education which are inconsistent with the new concepts being offered

Often a ToTs' role is to try to introduce participants to ideas about, for example, education deriving from different value systems. In such circumstances, ToTs need to respect existing values and help people become aware that they hold them. The point here is to model genuine respect and understanding for their existing point of view, while doing what you can to help them appreciate that there are other, legitimate, ways of thinking and that, if they are willing to make the effort to try and understand these, they will get a bigger picture of the elephant. Another maxim we bear in mind here is: *You cannot change anybody, you can only change yourself.* Remembering this has led us to realize that the only thing we can do to help those who seemingly 'don't get it' is to choose to say and do something different to try to support their coming to understand the alternatives. Ultimately, however, it is they who will have to decide whether or not they are going to try to understand you.

Contextual issues that make it difficult for participants to see any relationship between what is being offered and their own professional or personal realities

The ToT may be listening carefully to participants' 'Yes, buts' such as *'I have over 100 pupils, I do not have access to IT in my classroom.'* Reactions such as these (assuming a reasonably thorough needs analysis has been carried out) suggest that participants have been unable to see the principles underlying an idea 'grown' in one reality as being relevant and usable in their own particular other reality. This may be a case of not having spent enough time enabling participants to work through how conceptual tools and practical ideas might be useful to them in their own very particular contexts (Steps 4 and 5). Hearing this also tells you something about how those participants are approaching the course – perhaps still with an expectation that the course will supply them with ready-made ideas to take away and 'apply'. This could be particularly true, for example, if 'Yes, buts' come after the demonstration of a technique that participants think they are supposed to return to their classrooms and perform exactly as demonstrated. This may mean that the ToT needs to be more explicit about the purposes of the experiences and opportunities for learning that are being provided on the programme. In other words, say something like *I'm going to demonstrate a technique not because I expect you all to do it exactly as I do it back in your classrooms (though some of you may want to try), but because it is going to allow us to explore some of the conditions that help pupils to learn.* Given the nature of our attention spans, it may be necessary to make this explicit on many further occasions.

To judge learners' emotional state

This can be inferred from:

- how people talk – loudly, shyly, passionately
- body language – smiles, frowns, defensive arm and leg crossing, leaning back or forward (so here we are going beyond actual listening)
- less frequently – the actual words used 'panic', 'hate', 'excited'

ToTs need to pay attention to emotional states for several reasons. First and most practically for a ToT's work, evidence of emotional states can inform us about the appropriateness of the tasks/learning opportunities being proposed, in terms of the demand they are making: whether they are in fact scaffolding most of the participants or being too demanding or easy. Researchers (Csikszentmihaly 1990) have shown that, when carrying out a task, there is a relationship between people's perceptions of the demands of the task, their perceptions of their available skills to bring to it and their feelings. For example, if people believe that a task is too easy in comparison to their skills or knowledge, they will be bored. In contrast if they believe a task is too difficult for them, they may become anxious. Csikszentmihaly discovered that, when there is just enough challenge for people to feel the task is stretching them, and they believe they can rise to that challenge, people are in what he calls a state of 'flow'. In this state people don't notice time passing, because they are fully engaged in the activity and, while they may be pleased and content at having undertaken and completed the task when it's over, during it they are not aware of and do not express any signs of any particular emotional state. Therefore, when we detect evidence of sustained emotion in our learners during the learning, we question whether we have judged the challenge that the task represents for our learners correctly. An anxious learner may need to be reassured that they do in fact have the skills and knowledge to achieve the task, or may need the task to be broken down into a number of achievable stages, or be given an easier task altogether. We hope you can see the connection to scaffolding here.

The second reason why it is useful for ToTs to 'take the emotional temperature' is that, in any change process, it is normal to go through various general emotional states. The early stages of any new learning are typically characterized by 'uninformed optimism' or high mood, changing after time to 'informed pessimism' before gradually going through stages of acceptance, realism, hope and finally satisfaction at achievement (Brandes and Ginnis 1989). Groups as a whole, as well as individuals, are likely, at some point in the programme, to reach the 'informed pessimism' stage. We find that when this happens the only answer is to keep going (we find the 'Freddy the Frog' story useful on such occasions – see chapter 10). The ToT's roles as a motivator and reassurer are particularly important at this stage. So however far away participants seem to be and however despairing we may feel, we try not to let it show and remind ourselves as well as the participants to 'trust the process' and keep going.

The reasons ToTs think that emotions are important for teacher learning are, of course, the same for pupil learning also. The third reason for taking notice of learners' emotional responses is, therefore, that it provides an opportunity for ToTs to model doing so and thus model taking 'the whole learner/pupil' into consideration. Why is listening so difficult?

We've seen that accurate listening is an important ToT skill. Unfortunately, it is not as straightforward as it seems. Some of the difficulties involved in listening accurately are:

Head chatter

It is hard in any process of listening for the listener to keep their own 'head chatter' at bay. On hearing something a participant says, for example, we may find our own thoughts in response to what we hear distract us from actually continuing to listen to what is being said. Typical distractors for us might be thoughts like ' Oh yes, me too – that reminds me of ... I want to say it when I get a chance', or even 'Gosh, what a thing to say! I would never have thought *he* would say that!' and so on.

Mishearing

When we have been very involved in a particular idea or have a very clear idea of what we want or hope participants will say, we have often found we can mishear and 'hear' what we expect to hear rather than what is actually said.

Misunderstanding

Listening involves not only decoding sounds into meanings of words, but also understanding what the speaker intends to express through those words. There is a sense in which words do not 'have' meanings, *people* have meanings they want to express. So we have found ourselves hearing, for example, 'teaching' and assuming the speaker means the same thing by this as we do. (See our discussion of the different meanings behind this term in the General Introduction.) You may think that such misunderstanding occurs only when such 'big' terms are used, and this is certainly more likely, but we have had to question whether we share the same understanding of many more everyday words too.

Selective hearing

In a sense this is similar to mishearing as it has often been the result of too rigid an expectation on our part of what we will hear. However, in this case we have accurately heard some of what was said, but, because we didn't pay attention to all of it, we didn't get the full message. For example, we heard the first statement, but not the 'but' that followed.

The purpose of listening then is to understand the people and the meanings they want to express. We love the English word 'understand' because of the meaning to 'stand under', suggesting a need to put ourselves in the shoes of the other, or to see the world from their position. Whatever particular purpose ToTs have for listening, they will need to 'stand under' their learners in order to achieve it.

Conclusion

In this chapter we have suggested that if we were members of your ToT development group, we might offer to prepare sessions to work with the group in three areas – The management of small-group work, Scaffolding and Listening. (We would not, though, stand up and lecture at you in the way that, after reading the above, you might fear we would!)

Any one group of ToTs who gather together regularly may decide to spend all of their group life engaged in only one of the activities in Chapters 8 and 9. Fairly predictably we suggest that decisions on which activities and how often they are used will depend on the shared group goals that have been established during the group-formation stage. These will hopefully be based upon the interests and contexts of group members.

Chapter 10

Managing your development alone

It is a challenge to anyone to have to manage their learning alone, even when you understand something about how that learning can happen and have developed the skills to manage it. It is a challenge, because you do not apparently have one of the main 'conditions' for that learning, which is others with whom to interact. However, there is a sense in which you are not alone, even if you think you are.

First, you have your participants and possibly, or if ToTing one-to-one, your mentee(s). Just as in peer observation we said it was useful to have another noticer, so if you are alone you can devise ways to find out what your participants/mentee(s) noticed about your work and how they felt. This not only helps you manage your own learning, but also allows you to engage in a dialogue with your learners, which can help you to identify their needs. Ways you might get information from your learners may be more or less formal. They include:

- reaction slips (see Malderez and Bodoczky 1999: 34–6)
- more formal questionnaires
- asking for information and opinions from focus groups as representatives of the wider group
- spending a few minutes at the end of a class asking participants to tell you what they noticed and what they didn't and thinking about it afterwards
- asking participants what they liked and did not like, and/or what they felt they have learned, remembering to bear in mind they might be saying what they say to please you

With a mentee it is more difficult to obtain honest responses to such questions, whether in writing or orally, because you know who is responding and they know you know. Here, therefore, you will need to spend time getting to know them and letting them get to know you, to develop the levels of trust where they will feel able to be honest with you.

Secondly, you can participate in 'dialogues at a distance', through reading and interacting with books and articles (we provide some suggestions in the Further reading at the end of each Part). Using these as productively as possible involves:

- only looking for information when you have a clear purpose (you are looking for an activity or strategy to do something, or some specific information to solve a problem or provide alternative explanations)
- thinking about who the authors are, and what experiences have led them to their views (see 8.2.3 Reading groups above)
- remembering not to take anything you read as the 'whole truth' (remember the elephant), or even true at all for you
- remembering that no published author can be more expert on your context, classroom and your particular course participants than you are

Other means of managing your own learning include remembering to pay attention to and value those flashes of insight that may occur at any time, especially after or during leisure periods (because this is when your undermind will have had time to work on experiences that you have had). For us such insights often surface on waking, in the shower or swimming pool, out in the garden or on a walk. You might also occasionally want to use the idea of a journal, or mentor yourself through the five steps as above, or attend conferences with a purpose (for example to find out Step 3 information – what other theoretical explanations there may be, what other people believe).

Finally, we try (and often fail!) to be as patient with ourselves as we are with our learners. Perfection is *not* just around the corner, or even possible, but we keep working towards it.

Time for another story that one of us was told as a child by her father, who repeated it not that many years ago when she moaned about the impossibility of actually doing the job that she was engaged in at the time.

Any reader who does not know how butter is made, please read this before the story.

Note on butter making

Butter is made by churning (which means mixing and turning) full cream fresh cows' milk to separate out the fats. You are left with solid butter and a watery white liquid known as whey.

> *This is the story of Freddy the Frog. Freddy the Frog had grown up in a pond in the corner of Buttercup meadow. One day when Freddy was nearly a full-grown frog he decided it was time to go and have a look at the world. He hopped out of his pond and across the meadow – past Ferdinand the Bull (beeerrrr), under the five-bar gate, past the sheep pens (baaaaa), past the stables where Harry the horse was eating his hay (neeeeigh), past the cattle shed where the cows had just been milked (mooooooo) and into the farmyard where he heard another sound, a very beautiful sound. It was the sound of the farmer's wife singing (la, la, la) and it was coming from the open window of*

the farmhouse kitchen. Freddy hopped under the window. The farmer's wife in her kitchen was happy. The milk her husband had brought fresh from the cows was in a bowl on the table by the window. Soon she would make butter, lovely rich yellow butter for her family, but for the moment she busied herself with other jobs. Meanwhile Freddy listened to the beautiful song outside in the courtyard. He wanted to get closer and with one almighty jump jumped through the kitchen window and 'Plop' right into the bowl of milk. At first Freddy thought to himself, 'My, this is warm sticky water! It's more difficult to swim in than the water in my home pond. But it's nice and cosy and interesting.' And he swam round and round. After a while he began to get tired and thought to himself 'I think I'll get out now.' So he scrabbled at the side of the bowl, but the sides were steep and slippery and he could not get out. So he swam on and scrabbled again and swam and scrabbled but still he could not get out. And now he was frightened and thought to himself 'Perhaps I'll drown' (because frogs <u>can</u> drown, you know). But then he remembered what his daddy had told him. 'Son', his father had said, 'if at first you don't succeed try, try and try again.' So he swam and he scrabbled, and he swam and he scrabbled, and he swam and he scrabbled and every time he wanted to give up he remembered his father's words 'If at first you don't succeed try, try and try again', until he began to notice that a strange thing was happening. Parts of the water were clearer and less sticky to swim in. Parts seemed to be getting yellower and lumpier. He swam and he scrabbled with renewed vigour until eventually there in the middle of the bowl there was a big solid yellow lump and the 'water' surrounding it was easy to swim in. So Freddy hopped on the lump, hopped out of the bowl, jumped back through the window, hopped through the farmyard, past the cattleshed (moooo), past the stables (neeeeeigh), past the sheep pen (baaaaaa), under the five-bar gate into Buttercup meadow, past the bull (beeeeeer) and back to the comfort of his very own pond. And the farmer's wife? Well, she never did find out who made the butter!!

So why have we told you this story ?

This story reminds us all that there will not always be immediate access to support when things get sticky and it can be tough to have to deal with issues alone (and one answer to the question above, of course, is that, apart from the fact that we love the story, recalling it now has helped our own motivation to keep going with this book!) So at times we all have to motivate ourselves. We find that stories can be a useful tactic here and this one reminds us that usually persistence will help to make difficult things become easier. What we are *not* suggesting, however, through the telling of this story is that you should 'jump out of the milkbowl' of being a ToT just yet!

Conclusion: Making our engagement in our own ToT learning visible

We said in the Introduction to Part 3 that one of the reasons why we need to be engaged in managing our own learning was that we need to give our course participants the experience of 'seeing' someone do what we hope they will do. One of the things we are likely to hope that they will want to do (part of most ultimate goals of teacher learning) is continue learning about, from and for teaching. One of the difficulties is that, like teaching, learning is often a private activity and not always very visible. Ways we have tried to help our learners see that we do and are engaged in learning from and for our teaching have included:

- Making explicit reference to how we are drawing on previous experience to make decisions for this programme (last time participants said/did this, so this time I want to try out ...)
- Making explicit reference to how we use their reactions after a session to gauge the effectiveness of our work and also diagnose their learning needs for the next session. Just as in the 'scaffolding' example in Chapter 9, the son used the mother's comments as a diagnostic tool for deciding what information she needed next, so participants' comments together with our memories of the session based on what we noticed (as well as our plan based on programme aims) provide a basis for our decisions about what they need next. This then is one of the ways of staying flexible and responsive to participants' changing group or learning process needs.
- Making explicit reference to an aspect of our teaching we are currently working on and asking participants for help (for example one of us tends to give less than clear verbal instructions and in working on this aspect remembers one group who were asked to help by suggesting strategies through which the problem could be overcome – (they, for example, suggested always writing the instructions down on the handout, which we now try to remember to do).
- Taking participants to conferences, telling them about conferences, making it clear that we value the learning opportunities that they provide and so do go to them ourselves.
- Bringing in a selection of materials from our own private library with a brief introduction to certain titles (for example: 'This book is wonderful, I was so happy when I found it. It really helped me with ... ') to model that we do find the professional literature useful, and how.
- Telling our personal stories behind any reading texts we may suggest, in particular starting from an experience which prompted our learning swing and which the reading supported in some way, as in Reading groups (8.2.3) above.
- Genuinely acknowledging the insights that we gain through hearing other course participants' stories and perspectives (for example: the first time we heard somebody saying 'How do you do that with 120 in the class?' was a trigger to realizing just how important context is and, although we wish we had said 'Thank you', since this was a while ago we probably blushed and felt inadequate). Nowadays we try to welcome such 'Yes, but' challenges and trust that together as a group we can find ways forward, round or through such problems. Whatever our working context may be, it will always be more or less 'a given', and we have to try to achieve our aim within it.

- Genuinely acknowledging the insights we get into our own thinking through having to keep trying to communicate what we mean in often unplanned and unpredictable ways (for example: answering a question that really makes us think by saying 'Thank you for asking that question because trying to respond has made me think about the topic in a new way.' The starting point for the development of the 'pendulum' (3.2) came from just such an occasion).

The whole of Part 3 has focused on strategies you can use to support your own development as a ToT. This reminds us of one more maxim,

'You teach yourself'.

We see two meanings in this maxim. The first reminds us that we must be engaged in managing our own learning. The second points out that how *we* behave and what *we* model is an important part of what teachers will learn from the time they spend with us.

Another saying we have is:

ToTs need to be mad.

Again, we see 'mad' as having two meanings. The first is one of 'craziness'. We have found it is useful to be 'crazy' for two reasons. When we have been 'crazy', in the sense of behaving in unexpected ways on programmes, this has helped make the work memorable to the participants. Also, allowing our own thoughts to be 'crazy' in a creative sense has made it possible to combine ideas and procedures in new and appropriate ways for particular participants. The second sense in which we understand MAD is as an acronym of the phrase Making A Difference, since the whole purpose of any ToTing is to make a positive difference to the learning and experiences of teachers and their pupils.

References

Bohm, D. (1996) *On dialogue,* ed. L. Nichol, London: Routledge

Brandes, D. and Ginnis, P., (1989) *The student-centred school.* Oxford: Blackwell

Claxton, G. (1990) *Teaching to Learn: a direction for education.* London: Cassell

Csikszentmihaly, M. (1990) *Flow: the psychology of optimal experience.* New York: Harper & Row

Freire, Paulo (1970) *Pedagogy of the Oppressed,* trans. M. B. Ramos. New York: Seabury Press/Continuum

Kelly, G. A. (1970) A brief introduction to personal construct theory, in D. Bannister ed. *Perspectives in Personal Construct Theory.* London: Academic Press pp. 1–29

Malderez, A. and Bodoczky, C. (1999) *Mentor Courses: A resource book for trainer trainers.* Cambridge: Cambridge University Press

Tuckman, B. W. (1965) Developmental sequence in small groups. *Psychological Bulletin,* 63(6), 384–99

Ur, P. (1996) *A Course in Language Teaching. Practice and Theory.* Cambridge: Cambridge University Press

Vygotsky, L. S. (1962) *Thought and language,* (trans. E. Hanfmann and G. Vakar. Cambridge, MA: MIT Press

Willis, J. (1996) *A Framework for task-based learning.* Harlow: Longman

Further reading

Professional development

Edge, J. (2002) *Continuing cooperative development: A discourse framework for individuals as colleagues.* Ann Arbor: University of Michigan Press
Edge's work suggests a particular way of listening which represents an alternative way of working when sharing stories to the five-step/pendulum model that we suggest.

Burns, A. (1999) *Collaborative action research for English language teachers.* Cambridge: Cambridge University Press
Something we have not mentioned above, but another focus for a ToTs together group could be the reading, writing, preparing, trying out, reporting back on that is involved in an individual or collaborative action research project.

Head, K. and Taylor, P. (1997) *Readings in teacher development.* Oxford: Heinemann
This could be a useful source of possible texts (and related activities) for a ToTs together reading group.

Hoban, G. (2002) *Teacher learning for educational change.* Buckingham: Open University Press
This text could equally appropriately have been put in Part 1. He uses complexity theory to explain the interconnectedness of everything that needs to be acknowledged if there is to be effective educational change. Given the ubiquity of educational change, you might find this another starting-point text for a ToTs together reading group.

Wedell. M. (2003) Giving TESOL change a chance: supporting key players in the curriculum change process. *System* 31/4, 439–56
If you are prone to blaming yourself for all the difficulties and dilemmas you face, this article may help you see how at least some of the responsibility for such difficulties might lie in other aspects of the context in which you are working.

Group dynamics and working with small groups

Most of the references below are from our own discipline of language education. Perhaps because in language-learning classes people more obviously need to 'use' each other to practise the speaking skill, the field has for many years acknowledged the importance of this area. The practical suggestions in Hadfield and Dornyei and

Murphey do not focus particularly on the language education context and are widely usable.

Dornyei, Z, and Malderez, A. (1999). The role of group dynamics in foreign language teaching and learning in J. Arnold (ed.) *Affect in Language Learning.* Cambridge: Cambridge University Press

Dornyei, Z, and Murphey, T. (2003) *Group Dynamics in the Language Classroom.* Cambridge: Cambridge University Press

Hadfield, J. (1992) *Classroom dynamics.* Oxford: Oxford University Press

Houston, G. (1990) *The red book of groups.* London: Rochester Foundation.

Again lots of good ideas and discipline-independent.

Tiberius, R. G. (1995) *Small group teaching: a trouble shooting guide.* Monograph Series no. 22. Toronto: Ontario Institute for Studies in Education

This book has a university-level teaching setting, and is discipline-independent.

Resources of tasks, activities, games, procedures

Look at the titles we suggested in Part 2, especially those related to planning. Bear in mind the resources available in your own discipline/subject that you could adapt for use with teachers so that you are killing two birds with one stone by demonstrating an activity teachers could use with their pupils at one level, while using the general format to support teacher learning. For example in language learning there is an activity called 'find someone who' in which pupils are required to move around the room, asking and answering questions in order to find people who ... This can be constructed so that in carrying it out pupils must use a particular language structure. This could easily be adapted for teacher learning by changing what it is the participants need to find out about their colleagues (e.g. people who always use/never use a particular technique, have/do not have certain problems ...). As always in making such adaptations it is important to keep the overall aim of the session and part of the session clearly in mind.

Stories

Elbaz, F. (1991) Research on teachers' knowledge: the evolution of a discourse. *Journal of Curriculum Studies* 23 (1), 1–19

One of the early influences on our thinking about the storied nature of teacher thinking.

Lyons, N. and Kubler-Laboskey, V. (2002) *Narrative inquiry in practice: Advancing the knowledge of teaching.* New York: Teachers' College Press

An example of how these ideas have developed to recognize the use of what is now called 'narrative inquiry' in discovering and documenting what Shulman has called 'the wisdom of practice'. A clear connection with the importance of the undermind and experiential knowing!

Owen, N. (2001) *The magic of metaphor: 77 stories for teachers, trainers and thinkers.* Carmarthen: Crown House Publishing

This is one of our favourite sources. (For example, we adapted 'The Bedouins and the pebbles' in Part 4 from a story in this book.)

Scaffolding

Wood, D., Bruner, J. S. and Ross, G. (1976) The role of tutoring in problem solving. *Journal of Child Psychology and Psychiatry* 17, 89–100

This is the article in which the term scaffolding was first used in the sense that we discuss above.

Mercer, N. (1995) *The guided construction of knowledge.* Clevedon: Multilingual Matters.

On pages 66–75 he discusses a socio-cultural approach to human development, some of the functions of scaffolding in action and features of successful scaffolding in its traditional one-to-one sense, all in rather more complex language than we have used here.

Listening

Sources we have used for many years include:

Brandes, D. and Ginnis, P. (1986) *A guide to student-centred learning.* Oxford: Blackwell

Johnson, D. (1986) *Reaching out: Interpersonal effectiveness and self actualisation.* Englewood Cliffs, NJ: Prentice Hall

Rogers, C. (1983) *Freedom to learn for the 80s.* Columbus, OH: Merrill

If you look at any academic database/search engine (such as Google Scholar) you will find long lists of books on active listening. We prefer titles where 'active listening' is embedded within views of the person of the teacher. One such more recent title is:

Mortiboys, A. (2005) *Teaching with emotional intelligence: a step-by-step guide for higher and further education professionals.* Abingdon: Routledge

This book draws on the work of Gardner (Gardner, H. (1993) *Frames of Mind: the theory of multiple intelligencies* New York: Basic Books) and Goleman (Goleman, D. (1996) Emotional Intelligence: why it can matter more than I.Q. *Learning,* 24(6), 49–50) and sees 'active listening' as a skill displayed by someone with emotional intelligence. It contains some very useful exercises and activities that might be interesting to explore in a cohesive and supportive ToTs together group. Those based on transactional analysis theory will help ToTs who subscribe to the maxim 'You teach yourself' to discover more about themselves!

Conflict resolution

Books already referred to on interpersonal skills have useful sections on resolving conflicts. In addition, you might look at:

Mayer, B. (2000) *The Dynamics of Conflict Resolution: a practitioner's guide.* San Francisco: Jossey-Bass

This book, whicn is not about education or teacher education, nontheless offers useful ways of thinking about conflicts and suggests that conflict resolution requires a way of thinking about conflict (e.g. as having three dimensions: perception, feeling and action), a set of intellectual and interpersonal skills and a clear focus. A useful 'ToTs together' text.

Part 4

Assessment and Evaluation

Introduction

We have made assessment and evaluation the final stage of the book, because, if ToTs are also called upon to be assessors, these practices will be the final ones they will need to carry out in the teaching teachers' sequence of designing, planning, preparing, teaching, and assessing and evaluation. However, we hope it will become clear that, while the actual assessing and/or evaluating may take place after the teaching has finished, work on the form and nature of the assessment may need to begin much earlier at the design and planning stages of any teacher-learning programme. In addition, outcomes of evaluation and assessment procedures from a prior programme can be used in the development of the next.

Part 4 begins with a chapter on assessing the teachers who have been participants on a programme, and possibly their teaching. It includes some discussion of the processes of designing, planning, preparing and carrying out such assessments as well as of some of the 'dangers' and difficulties involved in doing so. The final chapter of this book addresses similar issues with respect to programme and ToT evaluation.

Chapter 11

Assessing teachers and their teaching

Introduction

Earlier in this book we've talked about the need for ToTs to be assessing the learners' progress, emotional states and current stages of learning throughout the programme, in order to be able to provide appropriate support or scaffolding and judge how to prepare appropriately for future sessions. This ongoing and constant assessment may be called 'assessment for learning' or formative assessment. There is another type of assessment more frequently or obviously found in all educational settings, which aims to assess learners' level of knowledge in relation to programme aims at the end of a given programme. This is known as summative assessment. The main focus of this chapter is on assessment that tries carefully to measure learners' level of knowledge at a point in time (usually the end of a programme).

Assessment of this kind often claims to measure learners' 'achievement', or the 'learning outcomes' of participation on the programme. However, this is not really possible in most cases unless there has been an equally careful assessment of learners' knowledge at the start of the programme, so that comparisons can be made between the two.

Before we go on, we want you to think back to your own experience. When was the last time you were a participant on a TL programme? Did you have to undergo an assessment of your learning on the programme? What was it like? What did you feel? What did you think was being assessed? Was there anything you learnt on your programme that wasn't assessed? Were you assessed on anything the programme hadn't helped you learn? Did you feel (or do you now on recollection feel) the assessment was a useful part of your whole learning experience on the programme?

If you are a practising ToT, what is the relationship between the way in which you assess and your answers to the above questions?

When faced with the need to assess, as with other practices, ToTs are initially likely to act according to their previous experience of being assessed or acting as an assessor of pupils. However, at times you will probably find yourselves, as we have, being required to be assessors in very different contexts or for different purposes from those you have previously experienced. Therefore, it is important to look at and try to understand some of the most common purposes for assessing teachers. Without being clear about what different purposes there may be, ToTs cannot decide whether replicating their previous experience of assessment will be appropriate for their present purpose in a particular situation.

Broadly speaking, and in addition to assessment of learning during and at the end of TL programmes of various kinds, there are two other purposes for which assessment of teachers commonly takes place. The first is at the end of initial teacher preparation programmes where assessment will normally also have a 'gatekeeping' function into the profession, and successful assessment outcomes are recognized as according some official 'licence to teach'. The second is the kind of assessment of teachers' classroom teaching that forms part (sometimes the only part) of a teacher appraisal system. Such appraisal systems may have two functions. One may relate to 'accountability': the purpose of assessment here is to check that teachers are performing more or less as expected, according to more or less explicitly stated contextual norms. A possible further purpose, arising from the first, may be to conduct a more or less formal needs analysis to identify common lacks/needs for further teacher learning, and so additional programmes, among groups of teachers in a particular context.

We believe that ultimately any assessment of *integrated* teacher learning (where all three types of knowledge combine) can only happen in schools. The assessment format and process will therefore need to take account of the context within which teachers being assessed work (considering, for example, the available facilities, the pupils' socio-economic background and parental expectations, or the degree of formal and informal support available). ToTs may also need to question whether it is actually appropriate for them (or other external entities) to assess teacher learning after a particular TL programme. For example, if the ultimate goal of teacher learning in a particular in-service programme has aimed to develop more reflective or professional teachers, assessment may not be appropriate since the programme message has been that participants need to assess themselves continuously, and the ToTs will have tried to teach (scaffold) them to do so. In such cases, external assessment amounts to 'doing it for them', at a point when, in scaffolding terms, ToTs might hope this was no longer necessary. External assessment therefore sends a contradictory message to participants on any programme which tries to help teachers to develop the skills and confidence to manage their own informed, evidence-based, and contextually appropriate learning.

In the real world, of course, we are aware that, since assessment is a taken-for-granted practice that is surprisingly infrequently questioned in terms of its impact on learners and learning aims, the above contradiction is very prevalent. Consequently, it is very often assumed that participants on TL programmes of all kinds should be assessed (partly because these assessments are often the central or only component of programme evaluations – see 12.1).

One way in which ToTs might try to mitigate the inconsistency between helping teachers learn how to assess themselves and encouraging them to do so as an ongoing developmental process, and then acting as an assessor, could be to involve teachers in the assessment process. Some ways of doing this (for example, through a portfolio, or through helping participants to understand and use the 'official' assessment criteria to contribute to their own assessment) are discussed below.

We will also introduce some ideas for how ToTs can deal with the many in-service programmes that are supposed to conclude with some immediate assessment of teachers' learning. Conclusions that can be drawn from assessment at this point are limited since teachers will have had no chance to demonstrate the shorter or longer-term impact of what they have learned on the programme on either their own teaching or their pupils' learning.

Before going on to consider how ToTs might approach the actual process of assessment we would like to explain in a bit more detail what we mean by assessment.

11.1 What do we mean by assessment?

Assessment is a process which involves gathering evidence of some kind on which to base judgements. Assessment is always, at least in principle, carried out for some stated purpose and, as an assessor, you have to bear that purpose in mind. We said above that there are several purposes for assessment. For example, one common purpose is accountability – are teachers doing the job they are paid to do to an acceptable standard? – while another is 'gatekeeping' – are we going to admit this person as a member of the profession and let them loose on our children? This need for there to be a clear purpose for assessment, usefully expressed as a question to be answered, is the same for long or short-term TL programmes. Therefore, if we think about a purpose for assessing our draft programme in Chapter 5, we might decide that it is to try and answer the question 'Can teachers who have attended our programme now use their textbooks with some consideration of learner needs?'

Another, often unstated, and very common purpose of much summative assessment of learners (on in-service programmes especially), is to gather evidence to use to evaluate the ToT or the programme, rather than to make judgements about the participants' learning or stage of development. So the first key issue here is the need to be explicit about what the purposes of any assessment are, and the second is to ensure that the 'questions' you try to answer suit these purposes.

In order to answer the questions, evidence will need to be gathered on the basis of which judgements are made. Such judgements are rarely just 'yes' or 'no' answers to questions such as those given above. More often they are made along some kind of scale. There are two main types of such scale. The most traditional scale is one in which each participant's evidence is considered against evidence from other participants to enable a rank order of performance/achievement/level of knowledge to be established. Ranking according to this kind of scale is termed 'norm referencing' and typically results in one or two of the participants being ranked as 'excellent' (in relation to fellow participants), a few 'good', a large majority 'satisfactory' and a handful as 'fail'. The problem with this way of ranking participants is that it is difficult to say anything clear about what those ranked at each point on the scale know and can do. Consequently we cannot say for certain that 'excellent' participants from one programme are similar to 'excellent' participants from another, or that a person who 'fails' on one programme, could not receive a 'good' on another.

A second way of trying to make a judgement based on the evidence that has been gathered is to try to match it against a predetermined set of explicitly stated criteria (see below). Such assessment is known as criterion referencing and it has several advantages. One is that it does allow statements to be made about what participants who meet the criteria at various levels can do and know about. Another is that it is potentially more transparent and fair, and it allows for standardization – all assessees are judged according to the same stated/public criteria. This is particularly important if the results of the assessment really matter, such as when we try to answer the above-mentioned question 'Are we going to admit this person as a member of the profession and let them loose on our children?' A final advantage of criterion-referenced assessment is that in order to establish criteria it is necessary to spend time thinking about what the criteria should be, and precisely what needs to be demonstrated to show that the criteria have been met. This makes it more likely that the purpose of the assessment has been (more or less) thoroughly thought through.

What then do we mean by 'criteria'? Let's look at a fairly simple example from the non-teaching world.

Imagine you are walking around a garden full of flowers trying to decide which to pick to put in a vase to greet your mother who is coming to stay. In order to judge the suitability of each flower you may take into account its colour, whether it 'goes with' the other flowers you have picked and the colour scheme in the room where you intend to place them, what you know about your mother's preferences, the vase you intend to use and how long the flower is likely to last, the size and shape of the flower and perhaps its scent. In other words, knowledge of your mother's likes and dislikes, the flower's colour, size, shape, smell and how long it will last, together with features of the context in which it will be placed (for example the room and the vase) are the criteria on which you make a judgement about whether you will use a particular flower or not.

Within each of these criteria there will be degrees of perfect suitability for the purpose that you have in mind. However, since tastes differ, you may judge a particular flower to be more or less suitable than we would, for the particular vase to be placed in the particular room for the particular purpose of pleasing a particular person. If, therefore, we want to be as certain as possible that we would all judge the same flower in the same way, we would need to spell out more clearly what we mean by 'suitability' for each of the criteria.

We feel there are some parallels between judging the suitability of a flower for our purposes, and assessment, for example that of the suitability of teachers to enter the profession.

- the room where you want to place the flowers could be likened to the context in which the teacher would work – the educational system and the kind of teachers that such a system wishes the teacher-learning process to produce (see 1.1 Possible goals for teacher learning)
- the vase is like the individual schools within the system
- the other flowers are like existing members of the profession within schools that are similar to the one in which the teacher will be working
- the colour criterion (going with other flowers and the decor) is like the extent to which the teacher fits in with (and may complement) the other teachers in such schools and matches the expectations of the broader context

And like the flowers there will be other more or less explicit criteria on which the teacher will be judged.

So what does all this mean? Any criterion-referenced assessment process, after its purposes and the question(s) it seeks to answer have been made explicit, needs to develop criteria and make sure that both assessors and assessees understand their meaning in the same way. There then needs to be sufficient time and opportunity to gather evidence on which to base judgements about whether the criteria have been met. If we return to the flower-picking analogy, these opportunities for evidence-gathering could include smelling flowers, looking at them, and placing them next to others that will go in the vase. Essentially what is happening is that the flower picker (assessor) is giving themselves a number of noticing opportunities on which to base a judgement decision, which is not finally made until evidence of a number of different kinds has been gathered. For flower arranging (as also too often for teacher assessment) this process tends to be carried out intuitively. While for flower arranging this rarely matters, for teacher assessment it does, since, if every assessor makes decisions based purely on their gut feelings, the assessment system cannot be fair, and it will be difficult to say anything consistent about the knowledge or skills of those who are judged to have 'passed'.

For us, once the criteria have been established, the stages of any criterion-referenced assessment process (including teacher assessment) are very similar to the five stages of the pendulum (3.2).

- Stage 1 is noticing. This relies on the assessor having had enough opportunities to notice evidence relating to each of the criteria.
- Stage 2 is interpreting that evidence in the light of the criteria.
- Stage 3 (when it exists) can involve considering others' interpretations of the same criteria (second marking), or thinking about one's own interpretations in the light of, for example, the contextually accepted ultimate goal of teacher learning.
- Stage 4 involves using all the work done so far to make a judgement of the

extent to which a teacher learner 'fits' each of the criteria for success and whether overall they 'pass'.
- Stage 5 is making the decision about what to do next in terms of what grade to give, whether or not to give a certificate, whether to let them try again or whether to make other specific recommendations.

Ideally (as we will discuss below) you as a ToT will be involved in the development of criteria. If you are not, but are expected to use criteria that have been developed by others, it is useful to be aware that these are not always called 'criteria'. In England, for example, candidates for the licence to teach are judged against 'standards'. In other places teachers may be assessed against a list of 'competencies'. Whatever the label, however, if the assessment process requires teachers to show evidence of their achievement in a series of pre-specified areas of professional behaviour and/or knowledge, in assessment terms these are criteria.

11.2 Planning for assessment

The results of teacher assessment may be more or less important for different levels of the education system. For example, within the wider education system a short in-service programme, of the kind for which we drafted an outline in Chapter 5, may be one important component of national-level planning to help teachers cope with the professional demands of a recently introduced educational reform. In such a case the outcomes of any teacher assessment may be seen as one important means of evaluating (see below) the extent to which such national planning and provision has indeed been supportive for teachers.

Here, while at a national level the results of the assessment may be one important element in helping the educational authorities judge whether their planning to support teachers is 'working', for individual teachers the status of the assessment might be different. The results might be personally important to the individual in the sense of helping them gain a sense of achievement and identify where future learning could be targeted. However, the results may have few career consequences, other than, perhaps, helping teachers to accrue some of the continuous professional development 'points' that may be necessary for eventual promotion.

In one-to-one assessment situations (such as annual inspections of teaching by official inspectors) the consequences of assessment may be greater for the individual teacher by, for example, directly influencing immediate promotion prospects. In initial teacher preparation, the final 'licence to teach' assessment clearly has major consequences both immediately for the individual and in the medium to longer term for the education system which the individual will or will not be entering.

Overall, therefore, when planning for assessment, programme designers need to consider how 'important' the assessment results will be, to whom they will be important and in what way(s). Broadly speaking, the greater the consequences of the assessment decision for individuals and/or the system (the higher the stakes), the more effort it is worth investing in planning and preparing, both before any assessment actually takes place and during the assessment process itself.

Before any assessment begins, aspects to consider relating to criteria and their use include:

- How much time and energy should be spent on developing criteria? Who should be responsible for doing this?
- How much training will assessors need to use criteria as designers intended? Who should provide this? Where? When? How much time is needed?
- What training in observation and noticing will assessors need? Who should provide it? Where? When?

During the assessment process questions to consider include:

- Is it necessary to get assessors together before they start assessing alone to agree on how samples of actual evidence will be interpreted against the criteria for standardization purposes?
- Shall we use more than one assessor in the decision-making process to increase reliability and fairness?
- How much time will assessors need for the reviewing the evidence, judging and decision-making processes?
- Once an assessment process is established (if it is large-scale and high-stakes), do assessors need to be brought together to try to ensure that criteria continue to be used in a more or less standard manner and to consider any adjustments to the assessment process that might be needed in the light of experience? How often ought this to happen? How long for?

As we hope is clear from what has been discussed, the first step in planning any assessment is to decide what its purpose is, what question(s) the evidence gathered during the assessment will answer. Once that has been established, the next step is to consider what criteria it will be appropriate to use to assess the evidence that is gathered to answer the question(s). In the next section we look at the criteria development process in more detail.

11.3 Criteria development

Once the question(s) to be asked have been agreed, developing criteria to help answer it/them is one of the first tasks in any criterion-referenced assessment process.

The process of developing criteria for any assessment will be strongly influenced by:

- the contextually agreed ultimate goal of teacher learning that underpins the teaching on the programme
- the actual programme aims themselves

Criteria for assessment of teachers are influenced by views of the ultimate goals of teacher learning (and, if the ultimate goals of teacher learning in your system are not explicitly stated, one way of finding out the taken-for-granted assumptions about these is to look carefully at how the assessment of teachers is currently carried out). Let's therefore have a look at what sorts of criteria might be consistent with different views of such goals.

Table 8 Example criteria and sources of evidence for programmes with different ultimate goals for teacher learning

Goals	Some possible criteria	Sources of evidence
'Good' Teacher	a) Interpersonal skills, including ability to empathize and develop productive relationships with learners, colleagues, parents.	School-based observation.
	b) Having a contextually appropriate 'teacher identity' (dress, commitment level, use of shared professional language, etc.).	School-based observation. Written statement of personal philosophy. Interview with colleagues and/or candidate.
Developing 'good teaching'	a) Effective in-class teaching which promotes learning (e.g. class management, scaffolding skills, assessing pupil learning etc.).	Classroom observations. Interviews with pupils and parents. Records of pupil achievement.
Teacher as a professional	a) Professionalism (e.g. evidence of involvement in ongoing learning, membership of professional community, etc.).	Journal contributions. In-service programme and conference attendance records. Interviews with head teachers or colleagues.
Reflective practitioner	a) Ability to notice. b) Ability to learn from what they notice. c) Ability to explain why they do what they do. d) Impact of such reflection on actual teaching.	Post-lesson discussions and subsequent classroom observation of lessons. Teaching journals.
Technicist	a) Ability to execute teaching plans as intended.	Classroom observation. Lesson plans, schemes of work.

Another way of generating criteria, and the evidence on which they can be assessed, is to think of the three types of knowledge. 'Knowing about' knowledge of whatever kind can be assessed through written examinations/assignments or oral presentations. 'Knowing how' knowledge can be assessed through micro-teaching demonstrations or classroom-based observations. 'Knowing to' knowledge can only be inferred by a skilled observer through classroom observation and subsequent discussion.

Having established broad criteria, the next step is to consider what precisely you would have to see/hear to be able to judge whether or not a teacher learner has, for example, the required level of 'interpersonal skills' (see first item in Table 8 under 'good teacher' above). This involves describing examples of the types of evidence that could help us make a judgement. This listing of examples is called developing descriptors.

The process of developing descriptors first of all involves thinking more deeply about what we mean by 'interpersonal skills' (as we have begun to do in Table 8 with the 'ability to empathize and develop productive relationships with learners, colleagues, parents'). Then for each of these components of a criterion a descriptor that details the kind of evidence that would allow us to make the judgement that the candidate had 'passed' on this criterion can be more easily developed. Taking 'interpersonal skills' as the example, and the component 'ability to empathize' we might find something like:

Pass-level descriptor 'ability to empathize'

Evidence might include:

1. Candidate talks about and seems to know and understand individual pupils.
2. No evidence of sarcasm, cynicism or derogatory comments observed.
3. Colleagues are happy to work with the candidate.
4. Candidate chats to a range of different people within the school community.

Based on the 'pass-level' descriptors you may want to elaborate further sets of descriptors for other levels of achievement, for example 'Excellent/Distinction' and 'Fail'. One of the difficulties in developing descriptors is the need to avoid moving from description to interpretation or even judgement. For example, in drafting the fourth descriptor above we moved from

> *Candidate has good relationships with a range of different people within the school community* ('good' = judgement)
> to *Candidate has positive relationships with a range of different people within the school community* ('positive' relies on interpretation)
> before settling on
> *Candidate chats to a range of different people within the school community*
> which we felt, if noticed by an assessor, could indicate the existence of a number of friendly relationships, as part of the evidence on which to make an eventual judgement about interpersonal skills.

Of course we are aware that people interpret language in different ways and that therefore different people will regard different forms of talking/behaving as 'chat'. This again highlights the need for assessors (especially in high-stakes situations) to spend time together, coming to agreement about what for them actually constitutes evidence of 'chat'.

> If you are using this book in a ToTs together situation, and you have access to Malderez and Bodoczky (1999), you might want to try out the activity Beer Bottles, Carob Pods, Conkers and Stones (page 123), to give yourselves the experience of this whole assessment and criteria-development process.

This process of elaborating descriptors for each of the criteria frequently results in a very long assessment instrument with which assessors will need to become very familiar, in order to 'tick or cross' the various boxes on the basis of the evidence that they gather. Despite all the hard work that goes into descriptor development, it is not at all unusual to find that once assessors have tried to use the instrument, they agree that not only is such a lengthy document unwieldy, but they are in fact making their final judgement and/or decision on an overall holistic impression of the assessee rather than on the basis of merely adding up the number of ticks on the assessment instrument. Strictly speaking this suggests that the assessors are using implicit criteria and therefore that the descriptors and criteria need revision.

This difficulty that assessors have in actually using very detailed assessment instruments containing a large number of criteria and an even larger number of descriptors has, in many contexts, led assessors officially to abandon the actual use of a cumbersome, lengthy assessment document in favour of a shorter, more holistic, list of standards, competencies or criteria headings, together perhaps with generic descriptors for 'excellent', 'pass' and 'fail' to be used with all criteria. Assessors *can* use these effectively, especially if they have all previously been involved in the descriptor-development process, which serves as a 'preparation of self' for assessors. These shorter lists can be much less effective though if they are used by assessors who have not had the same opportunities for preparation of self, and so lack a thorough shared background knowledge of the ideas and the thinking that lie behind the choices made about what to include (and what not to include) on the lists. How much this matters will of course again depend on the relative importance of the assessment.

The criterion-development process we have discussed is very time-consuming and costly and so is only likely to be appropriate for the assessment of high-stakes teacher-learning courses, most especially initial teacher-preparation programmes. Nonetheless, the kind of thinking process that is needed is relevant to assessors of programmes of any kind. If we go back to the short course which we outlined in Chapter 5, what criteria would we have, and what forms of evidence (given course aims and length) would it be realistic to gather and/or notice and assess teachers on?

The programme aims were stated as:

- to raise awareness of roles that textbooks can have

and, as far as possible, to help participants to

- develop the ability to assess their learners needs
- gauge the extent to which their textbook activities do or do not meet these needs
- begin to use supplementary materials and adapt or omit textbook activities where their analysis of a textbook unit shows that learners needs will not be met
- develop the willingness and confidence to continue experimenting with flexible textbook use

Based on these aims we developed the following question as the focus for our assessment:

Can teachers who have attended our programme now use their textbooks with some consideration of learner needs?

We then thought about what criteria to use to help us answer this question for each teacher. We decided on the following:

- ability to assess learner needs
- ability to use textbooks (adapted and supplemented as necessary) to attempt to cater for identified learner needs and evaluate the outcome
- positive attitude towards flexible textbook use and willingness to continue experimenting

Since this is not a high-stakes assessment for individual teachers (the consequences of 'passing' or 'failing' are not great), we decided not to spend time on developing descriptors for each criterion, although we did need to think about what they might be, to work out how to gather evidence. The most obvious and perhaps 'best' way of gathering evidence to answer this question would be for the ToT-as-assessor to shadow (or observe several times) each teacher using the textbook with their class. However, this would be very time-consuming and so costly, and unlikely to be 'approved' for an 'unimportant' assessment of this kind. We would therefore have to think of other less ideal, but more realistic means of gathering assessment evidence.

Something to bear in mind here, as with any assessment, is the desirability of trying to ensure that anything learners are asked to do to produce such evidence benefits them, in the sense of being a learning opportunity, as well as the assessors. The evidence-production process will therefore need to be designed to contribute to learning, as opposed to mainly requiring display of what has already been learnt.

For our course then some evidence on which to base assessment decisions could come from the following normal course activities, which were originally planned for pedagogical reasons and not for summative assessment:

- participants' reporting back at the beginning of the second block
- daily reaction slips

as well as from the following, which were included at the course-design/planning stages more specifically for assessment purposes:

- mentors' written comments about participants' ability to assess learners' needs
- copies of a number of lesson plans created during the school-based block, and a rationale for any changes to the textbook made

All of the above would provide some evidence, for a ToT who was prepared to notice it, of whether participants:

- noticed learner differences, and identified and were able to articulate learners' learning needs
- were able to act on what they have noticed in terms of how they use their textbooks
- are likely to continue the above once the programme ends

Another possibility would be to ask the participants to submit, at some point after the end of the course, a 'portfolio' which they felt provided evidence of their ability to meet the above criteria. In the spirit of *Never do for the learners what they can do for themselves*, and self-assessment this has some pedagogic advantages in that it requires the learners to:

- think carefully about the criteria, and
- select and justify the inclusion of the evidence they present

In our experience, depending on their contents, portfolios can be fairly time-consuming to assess and, on a short course such as this, a portfolio might constitute too 'big' an assessment task. However, if asked to complete these and hand them in one or two months after the course has ended, requiring learners to create a portfolio can help encourage the learning to continue for at least that length of time, and will allow more time for the skill of textbook evaluation and adaptation to become more automatic. For a programme such as this portfolio contents might include:

- a description of the class in which the textbook is being used, and assessment of learner/learning needs
- a general evaluation of the textbook
- a minimum of three lesson plans with a rationale for how the textbook is being used in relation to learner needs, plus post-use comments

Even though this programme assessment is small-scale and there will probably only be one assessor, the steps to be followed remain the same. It is important that the assessment criteria are clear to all (ToTs and the learners) from the start of the programme. It is also important that any evidence-gathering processes are fair and seen to be fair (for mentors' reports for example) and, if evidence is generated by participants, the same conditions are provided for all (for example the same support for the portfolio-construction process is given to all). Finally, it is desirable that the participants themselves contribute, in some way, to an assessment of their own achievements against the criteria.

Another way of thinking when planning teacher assessment, which is handy to use as a check of what you will have actually assessed if you go ahead as planned, is to consider what kind of knowledge the evidence that you plan to gather will represent. For example, written assignments of any kind, while the most traditional and easiest kind of evidence to gather (if not necessarily to assess) in many contexts, will principally represent what the writer 'knows about' as well as demonstrate their writing skills. These are necessary but not sufficient aspects of knowledge and skill learning on which to assess someone as a teacher or someone's teaching. Given that this form of assessment is so common, what can ToTs do to maximize its potential as a learning opportunity? Such writing is genuinely useful to teachers as an opportunity to 'articulate' and further develop 'articulation skills'. On a programme with an ultimate goal of producing 'professionals' able to write for professional journals the inclusion of this form of assessment might provide a learning opportunity. This would be so if, for example, on a module about using textbooks (part of a larger professional development programme), assessment through, say, a test, exam or traditional academic essay was replaced by asking participants to write a report, in a form that might be published in a named professional journal, in which they discuss their experience of trying to use the textbook in ways that are more responsive to learner's needs.

We hope it is becoming clear that for any course on which it is intended to carry out a formal summative assessment of the participants, the sources of evidence that will be needed for assessment purposes, for example time between the two blocks and provision for classroom observations by mentors, will have to be considered at the design and planning stages of course development.

Before we go any further, we would like to say a little about ways in which the very complexity of assessment of teachers and their teaching can, in a sense, make it 'dangerous'.

11.4 Reasons to be cautious

The first reason, touched on earlier, why any kind of assessment of teachers may be 'dangerous' is that, if assessment is not designed with care it may, as we mentioned above, undermine achievement of the aims of ways of thinking about the ultimate goals of teacher learning which expect the teachers to be able to assess themselves and their work. In such circumstances, if assessment is carried out solely by an assessor, this sends conflicting messages. One is that, despite the rhetoric, it is not really thought important that teachers can assess themselves. Another is that teachers cannot be relied on to do so accurately.

It is particularly when thinking about assessing in-class teaching through observation, however, that we see a number of reasons to be cautious. The first is that assessors can be 'wrong' in ways that impact negatively on the motivation of teachers. We have a real story to illustrate this.

> *One of us can vividly remember being 'failed' on an observed language-teaching lesson for allowing students to make mistakes during a period of 'free conversation'. The reason given for the failure stemmed from the then current behaviourist learning theory which held that language learning was a process of forming new habits and therefore learners should not be allowed to make mistakes for fear of forming bad habits. The language-learning theory on which she was failed is now largely discredited, so, although an assessor watching a video of that lesson today might still 'fail' her (this was very early in her initial teacher-preparation programme), the reasons given would be very different.*
>
> *A further reason for the affectively charged 'negative' memory of that occasion and the sense of injustice that she felt was that the assessor had not even bothered to ask why she had taught as she had. The assessor, she felt, had not understood that she had noticed what she perceived to be signs of boredom in the students and made an intuitive decision to stop 'drilling' (repetition of model sentences) and have 'free conversation'. This story highlights the desirability of ensuring that any assessment of teaching incorporates some sort of post-lesson interaction between assessor and assessee, in which alternative explanations such as the one mentioned above can be identified and taken into account.*

As usual, we have more than one reason for telling you this story. First, since ideas about various aspects of teaching and learning change over time, as greater understanding is reached about the processes involved and their complexity, it is unlikely that assessment of teaching can ever be an exact 'science'. The story also illustrates the negative memories that may result if both assessor and assessee do not share the same understanding of a set of explicit assessment criteria, or of the motivations for particular in-class decisions.

In Part 1 we suggested that teaching is a very personal activity, which in its early days at least, involves the establishment of a teacher identity. Negative assessments can therefore feel like an attack on that identity. This may be especially true today when current ways of thinking lead to assessment criteria that focus less on actual performance – the use or non-use of prescribed techniques and procedures (as in the illustration above) – than on more general and holistic ways of thinking and being.

There is also an issue of power in any assessment situation. First, the relative roles of the assessor and assessee inevitably mean that the assessor is the more powerful. The effect of feeling powerless may make it hard for the teacher to demonstrate fully what they can do. Another way in which power may affect the assessor's perception of what the assessee is capable of and/or knows, relates to the idea that 'knowledge is power'. The kind of knowledge that is most powerful in many assessment-of-teaching situations is the 'knowing about' knowledge of teaching, while the types of knowledge that are 'powerful' in the sense of having most impact on the activity of teaching are 'knowing how' and especially 'knowing to'. Assessors therefore need to be clear about whether they are assessing a teachers' ability to articulate ideas about teaching/learning (knowing about) or their ability actually to teach (knowing how and knowing to). Teachers' ability to do the former may not match their ability at the latter. If, therefore, assessors judge ability to teach mainly through a teachers' ability to talk or write about teaching, they may come to an inaccurate conclusion. This, for people who are better at doing teaching than talking/writing about it, may be demoralizing and/or frustrating because they are not able to use language effectively to defend themselves. Lortie (1975)* commented negatively on 'the impoverished language of teachers'. Although our understanding of teacher learning has changed since then, this attitude to teachers on the part of those further away from the classroom (and usually more powerful because of it) still largely prevails.

Secondly, much formal assessment of in-class teaching is based on the evidence from teachers' performance in a single lesson. This cannot possibly provide an accurate picture of the teachers' ability to support their learners' learning processes over the whole duration of a course. Consequently there will inevitably be a huge amount of information to which the assessor does not have access, similar to that discussed in peer observation in Part 3.

A final and important reason to be cautious about the form that an assessment process takes, is that this can have some very far-reaching consequences, and will influence what actually happens on a TL programme including the amount of effort and attention participants give to elements of it. This influence is known as 'backwash' or 'washback'. The backwash of any assessment on a course includes the tendency for teachers to teach to, for and like the assessment format, and for learners to value, pay attention to and give effort to learning only the kinds of knowledge needed to be successful in such an assessment.

Where assessment formats are designed in a manner that is consistent with the aims of the programme, and where, in addition to providing evidence for assessment purposes, they also have a pedagogical purpose, this backwash can be more or less positive (although participants' 'assessment anxiety' can still 'get in the way' of learning). When assessment methods do not 'match' the kind of learning that the programme hopes to provide (for example, assessment on a professional development programme for teachers, that only, or principally, measures 'knowledge about') the backwash effect can be negative. The extent to which positive or negative backwash matters again depends on the importance and value given to the outcomes of a particular assessment (or form of assessment) by the ToTs and the learners (influenced, of course, by the education system or society as a whole).

Having discussed the importance of trying to make sure that the evidence we gather is actually appropriate for our assessment purposes, as well as some reasons for being cautious when planning assessment, we now turn to look in more detail at evidence-gathering processes, beginning with the complex business of observation to which we have referred several times in the discussion so far.

---

* See References, p. 170.

11.5 The gathering of evidence – focus on observation

As you can see from Table 8 above (p.151), observation of classroom teaching can provide evidence against which to judge the extent of presence or absence of many of the criteria that we may want to assess. We say *can* because this largely depends on the skills of the observer. We discussed in Chapter 9 that listening (which can be understood as 'hear-noticing') is not as straightforward as it might initially seem. Classroom observation, in which observers are using both their eyes and their ears to gather evidence which they can subsequently use via interpretations and judgements to make their assessment decisions, is even more complex. Bearing the evidence-gathering purpose in mind will therefore be extremely important to any assessor–observer, because just as there are difficulties in listening, there are similar difficulties in see-noticing. As with observation in mentoring, the purpose of observation when used as an evidence-gathering tool is not to make on-the-spot judgements, but to gather evidence from which judgements may later be made. This is not as easy as it sounds, because in their daily lives human beings (including assessors) normally interpret and judge what they observe instantaneously, to make meaning of what they see. What they remember later are the instant meanings (judgements/interpretations) that they made rather than the actual visual or aural evidence on which they made them. If assessors behave in this way, their instantaneous judgements are almost certain to be based on their previous experience rather than on use of a set of principled criteria. The use of criteria requires the use of conscious (d-mode) mind, and it is extremely difficult to do this instantaneously or with any consistency while observing.

Just as with 'hear-noticing', so with 'see-noticing' too there are many assessor factors that may influence what is actually noticed. For example, the physical position of the assessor in the classroom will influence what it is possible to see (and hear). Their own preoccupations, biases and interests will also influence what they notice. People will always find it easier to notice 'mistakes' than the detail of fluent, seemingly effortless, expert demonstrations of integrated teacher knowledge. It follows then that assessors themselves need to be highly knowledgeable about the tiny components of fluent expertise to be able to notice them. All of these observation difficulties are compounded by the fact that there needs to be some method of recording observation, which means that attention is taken away from seeing (at least) what is going on in the classroom as notes are made.

The difficulties inherent in any attempt to observe the full complexity of classroom teaching in a principled manner provide a further reason for trying to elicit teachers' own perspectives on a given class, since together teacher and assessor might be able to construct a more accurate picture of what actually happened. In addition, of course, there are likely to be 30 or more other pairs of eyes in the room (the pupils) whose perspectives might also contribute to the construction of a 'full picture'. Even though a classroom observation might involve an assessor noticing what students are doing and/or what they are writing in their notebooks, the fact that pupils are rarely, if ever, consulted in such processes suggests that much classroom assessment in fact still assesses a teacher's performance at a purely technicist level and makes little attempt to assess aspects relating to the other goals of teacher learning.

What then do we mean by gathering evidence from classroom observation? An example we often use is of an observer who wrote 'boring lesson' in their notes. This is an example of a *judgement*. When we asked the observer what had led him to make this judgement he said that he saw 'bored children' – an example of an *interpretation* of something he noticed. When we probed further we discovered that what he had in fact noticed were three children yawning. There are many ways to give meaning to 3 (out of 32) children yawning. One possible interpretation is indeed that those three children were bored. If these children were in fact being insufficiently stretched, this perhaps indicates the need for greater differentiation of classroom tasks. Given that the other children did not yawn (show signs of potential boredom), then even if we can be sure that yawning signified boredom it would not be fair to judge the lesson as 'boring' for all the children.

However, there are many other reasons why children might yawn. Some might be:

- lack of air in the room
- post-lunch digestion
- lack of sufficient sleep the night before

Examination of other descriptive observation data might discover, for example, that a few minutes after the point at which the three children were seen yawning the teacher said *'It's a bit stuffy in here, can somebody open the window?'* suggesting that the teacher, at least, whether she had noted the yawning children or not, felt the need for more air. Or, in the post-lesson discussion with the teacher, when she described what she noticed, there could be a passage where the teacher talks about the three children struggling with difficult home backgrounds which might suggest lack of sleep or nourishment.

In the case we mention above the assessor in fact came to this judgement because *he* was bored. He had observed several teachers teaching the 'same' text-book lesson previously and, when he saw three children yawn, interpreted this to reflect his own feelings at the time. He was a novice observer and his reaction was extremely understandable for several reasons.

As we mentioned in the introduction to this chapter, all over the world teachers who become ToTs and/or assessors of teachers are likely to have received assessments of their own teaching in terms of the sorts of judgements that the novice observer/assessor noted down. Just as we tend to teach as we were taught rather than as we were taught to teach, so with assessing, unless we think about it and work hard: we will assess and observe as we were assessed and observed. Observation in both one-to-one ToTing (mentoring) and assessment requires observers to gather evidence of what they notice. Such observation requires a suspension of judgement during the process of observing and recording observations. In mentoring it is almost always the mentee who will be helped to make the final judgement based on the combined evidence gained by the mentor as observer and the teacher as noticer. However, since in assessment situations the final judgements are made by assessors alone, it is particularly important that these judgements are based on carefully matching accurate records of what has been seen and heard against standardized criteria, after and not during the observation,

It may be helpful at this point to try to explain what we mean by observation and noticing. Mason (2002) suggests that there are three possible scenarios. The first is that we simply don't notice something. This will often happen when people don't know enough about what is being observed to enable them to attach any meaning to things that are happening. Other observers in the same situation might know enough to notice more. An example of this would be spectators watching a sport which they have never practised, and which is also being judged by experts. Such spectators might wonder why one practitioner (ice-skater, for example) received a higher mark from the judges than another, when to them both seemed to do equally well. There was something the judges noticed that the spectators did not.

The second scenario is when we do register things at some level, but that the things that we notice do not make enough of an impact on us at the time that we notice them to make us want to talk spontaneously about them, but if someone asks us about them afterwards we can remember and describe them. This is most often to do with familiarity. There is so much anyone could notice that, quite reasonably, people save themselves valuable mental time and effort by simply not noticing anew what has become very familiar. The third type of noticing relates to things that do make an impact on the observer at the time when they notice them and that they consciously 'mark' as 'noticeable' and so are prompted to 're-mark' on (talk about). These are, for the reasons above, likely to be things that were unexpected or unfamiliar to the observer.

There are two main reasons why we think that this categorization is useful. The first is that because of the subjective nature of what any individual will mark, no two assessors are likely to gather exactly the same evidence. This need not be a problem if the assessor waits until later to assess evidence against the criteria. It can also help assessors develop their noticing skills, if they find later that they did not in fact mark sufficient evidence to make a judgement on one or more criteria. The second is that on TL programmes which have 'professional' or 'reflective practitioner' ultimate goals, it would be appropriate to assess a teacher's ability to notice. One way of doing this might be through gathering evidence in a post-observed lesson discussion, and remembering that what a teacher describes spontaneously about what happens in her lessons (as a result of a general prompt like *So tell me what you noticed in that lesson*) will tell you the kinds of things she more consciously notices and 'marks'. If she can give further information when prompted by a specific question, this indicates that a certain kind of (not very conscious) noticing was happening in the lesson. If she can't give any information even when asked (for example, about what a particular child did at a certain stage of the lesson), this suggests that she did not notice this at all, and possibly that there are gaps in her pedagogical knowledge in some way.

Noticing differs from observation in that it 'just happens', while observation takes place when an observer intentionally sets out to try to notice, always for some purpose. A ToT working one-to-one, may want to notice as much as possible about what is happening in a lesson in order to help the learner re-view (see again) the lesson and start a pendulum swing (five-step learning process). Noticing may also involve an assessor in attempting to gather evidence that will enable her to form an opinion of whether or not a particular teacher's teaching meets the demands made by a particular set of criteria. Although this makes it sound as though observation is 'planned', when you actually try to do it, you will find that all the above human difficulties connected with noticing still apply. It requires great concentration to stay focused on intentional noticing, even for the shortest of lessons. This provides both another reason why summative assessments based on only one (or even only part of one) lesson, are extremely suspect, and a possible explanation for why assessments are so often based on such very short stretches of teaching.

You may think it would be a good idea to video the class to avoid missing many of the real-time events of classroom teaching and notice 'at leisure' for assessment purposes. However, this can create its own problems. Having an assessor in the room can be stressful for the candidate. If then you add a probably unknown camera operator into what is already an assessment situation, it is likely to make the teacher even more nervous and stressed. If a teacher is stressed it causes them to be more 'self-aware'. If they are more self-aware, they are less likely to be able to make use of their intuitive expertise (their 'knowing to') since they will be more concerned with noticing themselves than with noticing their learners. When watching the video the assessor therefore needs to make particular allowances for the fact that they may not be getting a real picture of the extent to which the teacher *can* focus on the learners and the learning. Another problem associated with the use of videoed classes for assessment purposes relates to the fact that it is the camera operator who makes moment-to-moment decisions about what to focus the camera on, and therefore determines what can later be observed (and, often as importantly, what cannot).

The use of post-lesson discussions in an assessment situation, while desirable from many points of view, can raise problems of a similar kind. Such discussions are likely to be seen by the candidate as if they were an oral examination, which may give rise to two possible effects. Because they see it as an exam, the candidates may struggle to try to give answers and responses that they think are 'right' and that they think the assessor expects to hear. Also as such situations are stressful, the candidate may not be as fluently articulate as normal.

We have discussed observation of classroom teaching at length because it differs from other forms of evidence-gathering in that it is more obviously the assessor who must both gather the evidence and assess this. However, even when it is the teacher-candidate who 'provides' evidence (through written assignments, portfolio contents for example), the assessor still needs skilled eyes and a clear understanding of the criteria to notice the evidence that may be present for a particular criterion. The difference between 'observing teaching' and 'observing' documents of various kinds is, of course, that the latter can be done at comparative leisure, when contrasted with the challenges of gathering evidence from a messy complex lesson in real time.

Whichever method or combination of methods a ToT chooses to use to assess teachers and/or their teaching, the critical question to think about is 'will these provide enough appropriate evidence to make a judgement about achievement against the criteria?'

The world appears to be obsessed with assessment (we wish it was equally obsessed with teaching!), and we have only touched on some aspects of this complex field (see Further reading, p. 170) which we feel are particularly relevant to the assessment of teacher learning. As mentioned above, one reason for the ubiquity of assessment of TL programmes is its additional role in evaluating both programmes and ToTs. The results of assessments carried out principally for such programme or ToT evaluation purposes are then used to support decisions regarding the continuation of programmes and/or the rehiring or firing of ToTs. In the final chapter we discuss some aspects of evaluation.

Chapter 12

Evaluation

Assessment, as we have seen above involves making judgements about an individual learner's achievement, or understanding the stage they have reached on a particular learning journey. This may be a journey towards short-term goals (e.g. being able and willing to use a textbook more flexibly) or longer-term goals (e.g. becoming a (more) reflective practitioner). Evaluation on the other hand refers to a process that ends with an overall judgement about whether particular practices (leading to the design, the plan, the preparation, the actual teaching, the assessment) have been 'good' or achieved their purposes.

As you can see from the above we are using assessment to refer to judgements made about the work and level of the *learners* on any programme. We use evaluation to refer to judgements made about the work of *any of those involved* in any stage of programme development or any aspect of its actual provision. Making judgements about any/all of these people is often referred to as a course or programme evaluation. Such an evaluation will in fact always be making judgements about the work undertaken at each stage of the development process. However, in our experience this is not sufficiently recognized, and responsibility for the outcomes of the evaluation is most often attributed purely to the ToT disregarding the many others who may have played a part at various stages of the designing, planning, preparing and assessing sequence. Just as learners are not solely responsible for the outcomes of their assessment, if for example appropriate conditions and learning opportunities have not be provided, so a ToT cannot be fully responsible for a less than successful programme if appropriate conditions (including designs and plans) were not available.

We start by considering programme evaluation, before moving on to look at how ToTs can evaluate their own teaching in both a during-the-programme (formative) and end-of-the-programme (summative) manner.

12.1 Formal programme evaluation

There are three groups of people who may make or wish to make judgements about whether a course has been successful or not: the educational authorities or funders (who may or may not be the same people), the participants themselves and the ToT(s). Each of these will have more or less different reasons for making or wanting to make such a judgement, and will therefore need to gather different kinds of evidence to do so. It is the first group who are most likely to want to evaluate a programme formally, although they will need to draw on evidence from the other two groups to do so.

The only educational point of carrying out an evaluation of what has taken place, and what has resulted, would be to *look back in order to look forward,* that is to learn from the past to inform and improve what happens in the future. Unfortunately, however, in practice many evaluations are carried out and used more (or only) for 'political' or 'bureaucratic' reasons. While these reasons may provide the main motivation for the people or official body commissioning or carrying out the evaluation, they are wasting an opportunity if they do not also take advantage of the learning potential that evaluation affords.

Educational authorities and funders are almost always the people or administrative bodies who originally decided that the programme was necessary, and who may or may not have contributed to (or been fully responsible for) its design or planning. Their focus is likely to be on how successful the programme has been at achieving (or appearing to address or achieve) the purpose(s) for which it was originally funded and approved. To seriously evaluate a programme in this sense it is therefore essential to refer back to the purposes that were explicitly identified and stated at the initial design phase.

> If you go back to Chapter 4, you can find some of the designers' purposes for conducting our example programme explicitly stated in response to the 'Why' questions that were asked. If you look at the answers relating to 'lacks and wants' (for example, teachers feel they have to cover all the tasks in the textbook/ teachers do not know how to make decisions about which activities to use), we can see the original purposes for the programme.

How is it possible to find evidence of the extent to which the programme has achieved its purposes? One possible way is to evaluate whether or not the programme has made any difference to these 'lacks and wants' through a close examination of the assessment results of all the participant teachers (assuming that the assessment did in fact assess changes to such lacks and wants). This is a very common – and often the only – way in which the success of a programme is evaluated. However, this is a very limited perspective and it is useful to gather further evidence directly from the participants. They, whether formally asked or not, will inevitably evaluate any programme in terms of how they felt during it, whether they found it useful and whether overall it was worth their time and effort. Such evaluations may be important to educational authorities and funders at two levels. First, participants will spread the word. Their positive or negative evaluations of a programme will affect the attitude of colleagues who may be called as future participants to similar programmes. Secondly, knowing about participants' personal evaluations of a programme will help educational leaders to understand how participants are likely to approach their own future learning and how willing they are likely to be to participate fully in further programmes. Similarly the perspective of any ToTs responsible for teaching on the programme will be invaluable in terms of evaluating the extent to which the programme design and plan resulted in supportive conditions for the ToT to work within.

The types of evidence that can be gathered and/or examined for immediate end of programme evaluations include:

- open-ended questionnaires for participants and ToTs
- face-to-face review with some/all participants and ToTs
- evidence gathered for assessment of learners
- outcome of the learners' assessment process

However, as the ultimate purpose of any ToT programme is to affect what happens in schools in order to impact positively on pupil learning, a full programme evaluation may also need to take into account evidence gathered some time after the end of the formal programme. In such cases additional evidence may be gathered from:

- classroom observations
- examination of pupil assessment
- local supervisors or inspectors
- participants, and their colleagues
- pupils and their parents

Evaluation of other purposes for any programme or series of programmes, such as the issue mentioned in Chapter 4 about the relationship between teacher autonomy and willingness to remain in the profession, would again require a different kind of evidence gathering, and conclusions could only be reached over the long term.

For administrators, the outcomes of the evaluations will enable them to assess whether the original design and planning decisions that were made were appropriate and, if they are viewing the process as practitioners engaged in 'looking back to look forward', to identify their own development needs as designers or planners. In addition, if used for educational rather than political or bureaucratic purposes (such as for accountability, for the record, or because it is 'what you do'), outcomes will enable necessary adjustments to be made to future repeats of the programme and may inform the development of new purposes for new programmes.

For ToTs, participants' course evaluations can, as discussed below, provide a source of *some* evidence on which they can base their own assessment of their own work, to which we now turn.

12.2 ToT self-evaluation of their own teaching

Here we will discuss evaluation of ToTs and their work in both 'formative' (during-the-course) and summative (after-the-course) ways. The process of evaluating your own work, whenever you engage in it, involves asking yourselves and trying to answer four main questions:

1. Have the teachers learned what they wanted and what I wanted them to?
2. How far was what I did helpful or not?
3. How do I know?
4. What am I going to do next (time)?

Answers to these questions at the end of a programme, as well as any insights from the process and outcomes of a programme evaluation, can help ToTs to answer an additional question:

What are my learning needs and how can I address them?

which will genuinely enable them to use their 'looking back' to 'look forward', and possibly engage in some of the suggestions in Chapters 8 and 9 to begin to meet their identified needs.

12.2.1 Formative evaluation

The main purpose for ToTs evaluating their own work during the course is to manage the process of learning as appropriately as possible for their participants. Throughout any programme, we spend some of the time available between sessions using what we have noticed during the sessions, supported by participants' reaction slips to review (re-view/see again) our work. This in effect forms the starting point for 'self-mentoring' (see Chapter 7).

Typical starting points for such a self-mentoring/reflective process could be to consider when things during the sessions did and did not go according to the plan or meet our expectations. It may seem that when things do go according to plan there is nothing to think or worry about. However, even when this appears to be so we have found thinking about whether this is actually the case to be a very rewarding starting point for our own learning. Possible explanations that have occurred to us (our 'Step 2' of the 5-Step process, – see Chapter 3) when thinking about such a session later ranged from the possibility that it was indeed a pretty good plan, to the possibility that we had in fact been less responsive to emerging needs than we might have been. In deciding which, or to what extent either of these might be more accurate, we were forced to remember things from the session that we had not consciously noticed (marked). This process of forcing ourselves to remember has in the longer term benefited us in that what was previously unmarked for us (hard to pay attention to during teaching) has become easier to mark, so helping us, we believe, to develop our responsive observation and noticing skills. On occasions when our starting point was about something that did not go according to plan, our self-mentoring enabled us to work out what happened and what a possible cause might have been. For example, when we identified the cause as being to do with our plan, on one occasion we decided this was because we had misjudged how long our learners might need to complete a task (suggesting that we did not yet understand our learners sufficiently). On another occasion we identified the reason as being something to do with our management of the process, and so thought about our small-group management skills (see Chapter 9).

Other important formative evaluation starting points can include something participants said or did, what the products of group work actually were, or any other visible indications of how participants were thinking or feeling, either individually or as a group. It is on the basis of this kind of thinking that ToTs assess where the learners currently are in both group and learning processes, evaluate whether this shows the thinking or reactions that they expected/hoped for at this stage of the programme and consider what the answers to the above questions imply for what they need to do next in order to support participants' ongoing learning process towards achievement of the overall programme aims.

On the basis of self-mentoring (starting with some actual or recalled evidence and working through the 5 steps in thinking), ToTs can not only engage in ongoing contingent planning to support their participants' learning, but also become aware of some of their own learning or development needs. During the course there may be little time to pay more explicit attention to these ToT learning needs, but the engagement in and the outcomes of a summative evaluation of their own work allows ToTs to do this.

12.2.2 Summative evaluation

If formative self-mentoring has been undertaken, some notes, or at least memories of these processes are one source of evidence to use. Another is participants' evaluations. These, if you are free to gather evidence in whatever way you like, can be gathered through activities during the final disbanding phase of the course. Tasks in these final sessions will inevitably, through the reviewing of the learning process, require participants to summarize what they feel they have learned. A ToT can 'plan to notice' and record (or collect in copies of) the outcomes of such tasks. Similarly, ToTs can obtain some evidence of how participants have felt and are feeling through tasks which allow participants to 'review the experience'. In addition to this you may want to design a more formal written course evaluation/ questionnaire which can ask for programme evaluation purposes (see above) for participants' views of such things as the course accommodation, and facilities, as well as (for both programme and ToT self-evaluation purposes) teaching style, support, what they were most happy/unhappy about and what they feel they have learnt. If using this type of written evaluation, it makes sense to allow participants to respond anonymously and ask one participant to collect responses so that participants know you will not know exactly who has written what and so feel free to be honest. We often say things like *We are not interested in who is saying what, but want to get an idea of how you as a group have experienced this course to help us learn from this experience*. Paying attention to how you administer such evaluation forms is especially important, if these are completed before any assessment in which the ToT will act as assessor, as participants are likely to fear (despite reassurances and sessions on criteria) that any negative evaluation that can clearly be attributed to them might cloud the assessor's judgement.

Other sources of evidence on which to evaluate your own work on the course include:

- any comments from a team-ToT (see Chapter 9)
- your ToT journal, if you have kept one (see Chapter 8)
- handouts and session notes when looked at as a whole (see Chapter 6)
- collected reactions slips from each day or session

If you belong to a ToTs together group, it may be possible to get their help to use the evidence that you have collected to evaluate both what you did well and what your needs now are.

Finally, evidence of participants' learning (including but not confined to more formal assessment procedures), is useful in helping us evaluate our work. There is a kind of 'learning' that is rarely if ever assessed, and may be equally valuable to notice. We refer here to such things as: renewed commitment to the profession, increase in confidence, a more positive attitude, greater openness to different points of view, a greater ability to empathize, willingness to share, recognition of the value of belonging to a professional learning group, knowing where to go for support and further information and having the confidence to do so, and skills to use that information productively. We believe that these kinds of learning are just as, if not more, valuable than the more conventional and easily assessable 'learning' that tends to be most frequently referred to in any discussion of 'what participants have learned'. So as ToTs, it is useful to look at evidence of all these different kinds of learning when we evaluate our own work on a programme, and to think about what such evidence suggests about the personal development needs that you might address alone or with other ToTs in any available time between programmes (see Chapters 8 to 10).

Two notes of caution. No two courses, even if they have exactly the same aims and you plan to use the same materials, will ever be exactly the same because the context will always have changed. Time will have moved on and most importantly individual participants and so group dynamics will be different. Consequently, some types of evaluation of your own work (for example, *I spent too much/too little time on that*) won't necessarily hold true in the same way for other groups of participants even if you make no changes. What a ToT needs to identify is *why* they spent too much/little time (was it inappropriate monitoring, or poor task-design skills for example?) and what personal development needs the reason(s) reveal. So the outcome of this evaluation will not be to spend more/less time on a repeat programme, but instead to work on the development needs that have been identified. There is a sense, therefore, in which the learning which ToTs can derive from any post-course evaluation will relate principally to their own personal development needs.

Finally, whatever type of evaluation has been conducted, as we are all different personalities, some of those involved in TL programmes and their development will tend to see anything negative as 'all our fault', while others may be tempted to see problems as being due to less than perfect conditions or learners. Given that everyone involved in education at all levels is imperfect, the 'truth' probably lies somewhere between the extremes. This being said, *we cannot change others, we can only change ourselves*, so in terms of the outcomes of our evaluation of the course, it is up to us to decide what *we* can do, learn to do better or do differently, and then do it.

References

Lortie, D. (1975) *School teacher: A sociological study.* Chicago: University of Chicago Press

Mason, J. (2002) *Researching your own practice: The discipline of noticing.* London: Routledge

Further reading

Principles of assessment

Many of the specialist books in this area are extremely difficult to read. We have tried to keep our suggestions to ones that we feel are accessible to the non-specialist. Some of them are once again from our area of language education, but the sections we suggest that you look at are relevant in any assessment context.

Alderson, J. C., Clapham, C. and Wall, D. (1995) *Language test construction and Evaluation.* Cambridge: Cambridge University Press

One of the problems of much assessment is that it fails to state its purpose and to clearly inform assessors and assessees about its format and structure. The early part of this book deals with the process of developing clear test specifications that can be communicated to all relevant parties. Despite the 'language' in the title, the principles outlined are relevant to assessment of any school subject or 'teaching' as a subject.

Hughes, A. (2003) *Testing for language teachers.* Cambridge: Cambridge University Press

Again, although the title suggests a specific orientation, the chapters on basic assessment principles (e.g. reliability and validity) are particularly accessible to readers of any background.

Gipps, C. (1994) *Beyond testing: Towards a theory of educational assessment.* London: Falmer

This book provides an introduction to, and rationale for 'alternative' assessment practices – those which go beyond summative written exams or testes – such as peer assessments, self-assessment and portfolio construction.

Darling-Hammond, L. and Snyder, J. (2000) Authentic assessment of teaching in context. *Teaching and Teacher Education* 16, 523–45

This article considers 'alternative assessment' of teachers and teaching, and the contexts of programmes where these have been more or less successful.

Standards

Standards (criteria) for qualified teacher status in England can be found at:
http://www.tda.gov.uk/partners/ittstandards/standards.aspx

Evaluation

The *Evaluation Cookbook*, which can be found at:
http://www.icbl.hw.ac.uk//ltdi/cookbook/contents.html
offers suggestions for the planning, design, implementation and analysis of a range of strategies for both assessment (as we have used it here) and evaluation.

Observation

Apart from John Mason's 2002 book (to which we refer in previous Parts), you might like to look at A. Malderez (2003) Key concepts: observation. *English Language Teaching Journal* 57(2), 179–81 which briefly discusses the various purposes for which observation of teaching is currently used in education.

Final thoughts

We expect it will come as no surprise if we say that this joint endeavour providing as it has the opportunity for articulation, reflection, peer mentoring and team writing, has been an extremely valuable learning opportunity for us. You will have noticed that, despite some attempts to see the elephant from many different points of view, this book is written from a particular standpoint. Our standpoint means that, if you have come to this with a strong theory–application orientation, you will no doubt have found yourself saying 'Yes, but' on many pages. However, we too would have some 'Yes, buts' if you were to say that everything we have written is completely appropriate for your context.

Our point here is that this book describes *one* approach to teaching teachers. It tries to provide some ways of thinking that we have found useful in such work in the varied contexts in which we have found ourselves. Whether you find our ways useful in your context, or not, the questions this book has raised are ones to which any ToT, anywhere, working with any teachers, will need to keep returning. These include:

- How do teachers learn? (and how do I know?)
- What is the ultimate goal for teaching teachers in my context? (and how do I know?)
- What do the teachers with whom I am working want and need to know? (and how do I know?)
- What kinds of programme design best supports teacher learning in my context (and how do I know?)
- What can I as a ToT do to support their learning? (and how do I know?)
- How can I become a better manager of my own and others' learning? (and how do I know?)
- What is the effect of what I do as a ToT? (and how do I know?)
- How can I assess teachers/teaching in beneficial and supportive ways? (and how do I know?)

Whatever your view of what we have written, we have found that being a ToT, while being very hard work, can be hugely enjoyable and rewarding. We highly recommend it and hope you enjoy it too.

As we said in the General Introduction we have seen the reader/writer relationship as a form of dialogue at a distance. So far *we* have not heard the reader part of the dialogue and we would love to hear about your actual 'Yes, buts' and any other experiences that you have had, perhaps as a result of using what you have read here. Our email addresses are:

a.malderez@education.leeds.ac.uk
m.wedell@education.leeds.ac.uk

We leave you with one last story ...

Some Bedouin were on a journey through the desert. Night had fallen and they were lying on their sleeping mats in the oasis gazing at the star-studded skies, when all of a sudden they noticed that a light was appearing in the skies. It was so bright that the stars faded. They knew this portended a message from the Gods, and sure enough from out of the sky boomed a loud voice which said 'Go into the desert, collect pebbles, and tomorrow you will be excited, disappointed, and very, very curious'. And the voice stopped, the light faded and, as the stars reappeared, the Bedouins looked at each other and grumbled. 'What kind of a message was that? Why didn't the Gods tell us something useful like how to irrigate the desert or cure AIDS?' *Some were so disappointed that they did not bother to go and do as the voice had instructed. Others dutifully and more or less enthusiastically wandered a little way from the oasis, picked up a few pebbles, slung them into their camel bags, and went back to sleep.*

The next night at the next oasis, as the Bedouin were getting their sleeping mats out from their camel bags, one of them touched one of the pebbles that he had thrown in there the night before. He pulled it out and realized that on the journey it had cracked in two. He noticed something sparkling and, as he looked closer, became more and more excited. He called his fellow travellers and said 'Look, Look!' In excitement they gathered round and stared astonished at the diamond that had been uncovered. In excitement they rushed to their own saddle bags but their disappointment grew, as searching frantically they realized that they either had no pebbles at all or had only collected a few.

As they lay down later that night with the four diamonds that they had together found in all the pebbles that they had collected, they discussed the marvels of nature and one said, 'Who would have thought that these little brown insignificant pebbles could have something so precious at the centre?' and another mused sleepily 'I wonder whether, if we looked very closely, there might be more treasures to be found in all the seemingly insignificant things around us?' And so they became very, very curious.

(Adapted from Owen 2001, see p. 139)

Index